THE GRAND PANJANDRUM

MELLOW YEARS
OF
JUSTICE HOLMES

By

JOHN S. MONAGAN

UNIVERSITY
PRESS OF
AMERICA

Lanham • New York • London

University Press of America,® Inc.

4720 Boston Way
Lanham, MD 20706

3 Henrietta Street
London WC2E 8LU England

Library of Congress Cataloging-in-Publication Data

Monagan, John S.
The grand panjandrum.

Includes bibliographies and index.
1. Holmes, Oliver Wendell, 1841–1935. 2. Judges—
United States—Biography. I. Title.
KF8745.H6M66   1988   347.73'2634 [B]   87–34628 CIP
                 347.3073534 [B]
ISBN 0–8191–6853–X (alk. paper)

All University Press of America books are produced on acid-free
paper which exceeds the minimum standards set by the National
Historical Publications and Records Commission.

FOR
WILL PETER JOHN AND MATTHEW

Thanksgiving

Warm thanks to Erika Chadbourn, curator of manuscripts, emerita, at Harvard Law School Library for technical assistance, valuable advice and support; to Molly Adams, widow of Mark Howe, for helpful insights and encouragement; to Eugene C. Gerhart, editor-in-chief of the *New York Bar Journal,* for stimulation and productive counsel; to Professor David H. Burton, of St. Joseph University, and Kenneth W. Thompson, director of the Miller Center of Public Affairs at the University of Virginia, for guidance and backing, and to Florence Hollister, Michael Janeway and John Knox for rewarding cooperation.

A bow to Evelyn Bence for painstaking editing and scores of helpful suggestions; to Brian Cashell, economist, and to the Library of Congress for assistance in salary and income calculations; to Professor Harry S. Martin, III, librarian of the Harvard Law School Library and Judith W. Mellins, manuscript associate, for cheerful assistance in research, and to John B. Breslin, S.J., Jeremiah S. Buckley, Esq., and Rosemary Monagan for reading the manuscript and making valuable suggestions for improvement.

An obeisance to the memory of the late Judge Harry C. Shriver, long a Holmes devotee, for his interest and example.

Deepest appreciation also to all who cheerfully and eagerly talked with me about Fanny and Wendell and whose names appear throughout this book.

J.S.M.

The author is grateful for the permissions which follow.

Quotations from Howe, *Holmes-Pollock Letters* (1941), Howe, *Holmes-Laski Letters* (1953), Howe, *Justice Holmes, The Shaping Years,* and Howe, *Justice Holmes, The Proving Years* (1963) are reprinted by permission of Harvard University Press.

Excerpts from *Oliver Wendell Holmes, Jr., Papers, Harvard Law School Library,* the Sheehan letters of the *Holmes-Sheehan Correspondence* and the following writings of W. Barton Leach: "Meeting of Holmes Secretaries," *Recollections of a Holmes Secretary* and "Notes for a Talk on O.W.H." 1931, Harvard Law School Library are published by permission of Professor Harry S. Martin, III, librarian of Harvard Law School.

Excerpts from the unpublished diary of Mark DeWolfe Howe are published by permission of Mary (Howe) Adams.

Excerpts from *Holmes' Appointment to the United States Supreme Court* are published by permission of Professor John A. Garraty.

The excerpt from *Among Friends: Personal Letters of Dean Acheson* is quoted by permission of David C. Acheson, Esq.

The illustration portraying Fanny Dixwell is republished by permission of Deborah Gavel, the artist.

The illustration portraying Lady Castletown and Wendell is republished by permission of Jamie Hogan, the artist.

Excerpts from the Holmes letters of the *Holmes-Sheehan Correspondence* are published by permission of Joseph J. Casino, the archivist of St. Charles Seminary, and Professor David H. Burton, the editor.

Excerpts from Wister, *Roosevelt, The Story of A Friendship,* are printed by permission of Frances Wister Stokes.

Excerpts from Biddle, *Mr. Justice Holmes,* are printed by permission of Edmund R. Biddle. Excerpts from Biddle, *A Casual Past* are printed by permission of Edmund R. Biddle and Doubleday and Company.

FANNY HOLMES AT TWENTY-EIGHT. Artist Deborah Gavel's concept of the youthful Fanny Dixwell, a reconstruction made difficult by Fanny's photophobia and the consequent dearth of photographs.

Contents

Foreword

Justice Benjamin Cardozo called him "the great overlord of the law and its philosophy."[1] Dean Charles E. Clark[2] of the Yale Law School described him as "America's most loved and respected man of law." As a young man he had fought for three years as an infantry officer and had been wounded three times in battle. In 1931, his ninetieth birthday was a national celebration. As a legal scholar who wrote *The Common Law,* a monumental work in jurisprudence, he won the respect of juridical experts throughout the world.[3] As a member of the Supreme Judicial Court of Massachusetts for twenty years and of the Supreme Court of the United States for nearly thirty, he wrote opinions that struck stirring blows for individual rights and legislative freedom. The language of his opinions was brilliant and memorable. Justice Oliver Wendell Holmes, Jr., was one of the greatest judges in the history of Anglo-American law. At his burial in Arlington National Cemetery, President Franklin Delano Roosevelt stood bare-headed in the March cold and sleet to symbolize the esteem the nation felt for this noble warrior.

During his long life, Holmes received the tribute of honorary degrees, service awards, laudatory newspaper and magazine articles and national radio programs. Pundits in legal journals commented on his opinions and his judicial philosophy. He left a substantial body of articles and speeches and a spectacular volume of correspondence. Several biographers have dealt with his life and his exploits have even been put into melody in a recent musical, *The Yankee Belle,* by Ben Victor.[4]

In spite of all this exposure, Wendell Holmes, as he was known to his family, has remained a remote figure, strangely lacking in vitality to those who knew him only secondhand. On the printed page, the gusto of his vibrant personality has been filtered out, his charm, earthiness, and passion for life have been only vaguely or indirectly transmitted.

There are several reasons for the incompleteness of Holmes's picture—not the least of which was the attitude of

Wendell himself. As a New Englander and a Boston Brahmin, he inherited a regional reticence about personal matters and a sensitivity to manners and the proprieties of position. His Boston was not a swinging city and the *mores* of the day posited restraint. It was no accident that the first definitive article on the right to privacy was published in Cambridge in the *Harvard Law Review*.[5] Holmes gradually created his own world and was increasingly content to live within its confines. He complained several times to Professor Harold Laski,[6] the British scholar and a prolific correspondent, about people who sought his autographed picture—although he willingly gave such to his intimates. And his uneasiness about sexual explicitness in novels indicates that he would have deplored the current no-holds-barred biographies.[7] In his time on the bench, the accepted judicial code imposed a stronger limitation upon personal revelation.

In addition to his inbred reserve, Wendell knew exactly what type of figure he wished to cut with posterity. Mark De Wolfe Howe, one of his secretaries and later his biographer, says that Wendell carefully destroyed an appreciable number of his Civil War letters to his family and that none of the wartime letters to him from his parents have been preserved. Alger Hiss, also a secretary of Holmes, has asserted that Wendell wanted his letters to Harold Laski destroyed—several times seeking assurance from Laski that his wish be carried out. Laski, however, flattered the old man with protestations that he wanted to keep the correspondence with him a bit longer; he preserved the letters and made them available for publication in two volumes in 1953.

Wendell might well have wished to avoid publication of these missives because they contain frank and sometimes sharply critical appraisals of prominent lawyers and judges, his preference for Coolidge and Hoover over their opposing presidential candidates, John W. Davis and Alfred E. Smith, and his brutal description of the role of the common man. Further evidence of his desire to maintain a sanitized record of his life is his destruction of letters from his beloved friend, Lady Castletown, and his admonition to her to do the same with his sometimes emotional correspondence.

Wendell's determination to mold the elements of posterity's picture of his military career even led him to conspire in the concealment of events which he felt showed him to have been less than a paragon of heroism in battle. From extensive research, William A. Gifford, a painstaking and industrious student of Holmes's career, has concluded that Wendell "moved heaven and earth to suppress during his own lifetime . . . that [he] was saved from certain death at the battle of Ball's Bluff by young [Gustave] Magnitzky, then a private under Lt. Holmes' command."

Magnitzky was a young, German-speaking, Polish immigrant from Prussia whose many outstanding acts of bravery raised him to the rank of captain by the end of the war. Pursuant to an apparent pact between him and Wendell, even many years later when he recounted the events of the battle on the Potomac, Magnitzky failed to mention his rescue of the unconscious Wendell in the Union retreat. As a reward for his loyalty and valor, Magnitzky was brought into the firm of Shattuck, Holmes and Munroe where he acted as bookkeeper and "general boss." He spent the rest of his life in that firm looking after the Holmes interests in trusts, investments and properties.

The Magnitzky family who furnished Gifford this information also revealed that each year on his birthday, Wendell would send Magnitzky a year's supply of the finest Havana cigars and that each month, a barrel of Magnitzky's favorite German beer was delivered to his home at Jamaica Plain. In Gifford's judgment, this was Wendell's "way of commemorating the event with the rationale that but for Magnitzky, he would have no birthdays to celebrate.

Wendell felt that general knowledge of his rescue would detract from the mystique of his popular reputation for heroism during the Civil War. Gifford adds:

At one point, Magnitzky ran for a seat on the Boston School Committee and one of the Boston papers revealed the facts concerning the saving of Holmes' life at Ball's Bluff. Holmes reacted quite out of character (as the popular mind likes to interpret that character still) by flying into violent rage against Magnitzky's son Paul who had apparently mentioned it to a gentleman from the press without knowing he was not supposed to.

Wendell had his share of votaries whose attentions he enjoyed and encouraged. Many of these supporters were liberals

xi

and welcomed the accession of this Yankee Republican to their side on social and economic questions, even though, in fact, Wendell's openness was based upon skeptical permissiveness toward legislative experimentation rather than upon convinced philosophy. Laski called him "one of the greatest conservatives who ever sat upon that illustrious body." The adulation of these men limited full revelation of the complex personality of Holmes because they tended to enshrine him and give him greater than human dimensions. Among them were Harold Laski, Felix Frankfurter, professor at Harvard Law School and later justice of the Supreme Court, Jerome Frank, federal judge and author of *Law and the Modern Mind,* and Max Lerner, author and editor. Frankfurter said that Holmes was "Plato's 'philosopher become king.'" Francis Biddle, a secretary of Holmes and later attorney general of the United States, lamented that Holmes's figure "in its vigor and maturity" was not realized by the younger generation. Biddle maintained that Holmes should be "rescued from the adulation which has blurred the sharpness of his reality."[8] Valid as his analysis was, even Biddle's own biographical study betrayed the sense of distance between a devotee and the object of his veneration.

Unfortunately, the sharpening of the reality to which Biddle referred has not been achieved. Through their conscious or unconscious collaboration with their subject the true believers preserved a desiccated and decorous image of Holmes. The fact that he was ninety before biographies began to appear undoubtedly contributed to the inclination of commentators to treat Holmes as superhuman. In fact, one biography by Katherine Drinker Bowen was actually called *Yankee from Olympus.*[9]

In reality, Holmes was an intensely human person who knew violence and passion as well as contemplation and calm; he experienced sympathy, commiseration, and compassion as well as detachment and ratiocination It is this Holmes that the following pages are designed to reveal. And, since his earlier years have been studied in detail, I've directed my attention to the later truly mellow years.

As a concomitant to this closer look at Holmes, I've discovered the role Holmes's wife of nearly fifty-seven years, Fanny Bowditch Holmes, played in his life. Witty, talented, understanding, and eccentric in New England fashion, she was a considerable figure in her own right and provided Holmes essential support at critical times in his career.[10] Without her, his life would have been very different and probably less noteworthy.[11] As Holmes's picture is developed, the part Fanny played in creating this image will be given due attention.

NOTES ON FOREWORD

[1] Benjamin N. Cardozo, "Mr. Justice Holmes," *Harvard Law Review,* 44:682 at 691.

[2] Charles Edward Clark (1889–1963), lawyer, Sterling Professor of Law and dean at Yale Law School, local judge, judge and chief judge of U.S. Circuit Court of Appeals, Second Circuit. Outstanding figure in revision of rules of practice and procedure in U.S. courts.

[3] Sir Frederick Pollock, *Saturday Review,* 11 June 1881, p. 78. See also 25 *Journal of Jurisprudence* 646 (Scotland) 1881.

[4] Ben Victor, New York writer and composer, last known seeking angels for *Yankee Belle.*

[5] Brandeis and Warren, "The Right to Privacy," 4 *Harvard Law Review* 193 (1890).

[6] Harold Joseph Laski (1893–1950), British political scientist, author of *The American Presidency,* prominent figure in the Labour party, lectured at McGill and Harvard and taught at the University of London. Friend of Felix Frankfurter and Wendell. Writer of obsequious and not always accurate letters to Wendell in two volumes published as: Mark DeWolfe Howe, ed., *Holmes-Laski Letters* (Cambridge: Harvard University Press, 1953).

[7] James Bishop Peabody, ed., *The Holmes-Einstein Letters* (New York: Macmillan, St. Martin's Press, 1964), 3 vol.

He was no prude and wrote to Lewis Einstein about varying his more serious reading "with pauses for an occasional Can-Can in the way of some French indecency" (vol. 1, p. 23).

He also told Einstein that George Sand was "too solemnly virginal in her fornication to suit me" (vol. 1, p. 39).

[8] Francis Biddle, *Mr. Justice Holmes* (New York: Charles Scribner's Sons, 1942), p. 1.

[9] Catherine Drinker Bowen, *Yankee from Olympus* (Boston: Little, Brown and Company, 1944).

[10] Mark DeWolfe Howe, *Justice Holmes: The Proving Years—1870–1882* (Cambridge: Harvard University Press, Belknap Press, 1963), p. 96 et seq. 253–54.

[11] See also John S. Monagan, *"The Enigmatic Fanny Holmes,"* The Boston *Globe Magazine,* 29 November 1981, p. 14.

Wendell

In 1933, as he approached his ninety-second birthday Oliver Wendell Holmes, Jr., was known and beloved by the American people. As a citizen of the District of Columbia, he did not vote in the presidential election of 1932, nor did he support the successful candidate. His sympathies were with the retiring president who carried the Republican banner. Nevertheless, the advent of the Roosevelt administration was bringing many devotees of Wendell to Washington to play important roles in formulating policy; his opinions would be advanced to justify the passage of many of the laws they were to propose.

For this and many other reasons, Wendell had become a venerated national personality and, therefore, it was wholly proper that President Franklin Roosevelt, four days after his inaugural, should make a call on Wendell on his ninety-second birthday. Stimulated by Felix Frankfurter, a close advisor, F.D.R. warmly agreed to the suggestion. Donald Hiss,[1] Wendell's current secretary, had been warned of the visit two days before and had admitted the secret service men to test the elevator. He relates the subsequent events:

> On the birthday, we had a luncheon. Tommy Corcoran[2] and Felix Frankfurter[3] were there. I had gone to a bootlegger and gotten some champagne. Holmes loved it. "It feels good to your face," he said. Felix had ordered all telephone calls for him to be refused and we later found out that Marvin McIntyre,[4] one of the president's secretaries had been trying to get him so that F.D.R. could offer him the solicitor generalship—which he later turned down.
>
> At any rate, we had a very good and very festive luncheon. Then Tommy and Felix went their ways. I read to the justice and then he went back in his alpaca coat and dozed while I looked out for the president from the front windows. Finally, I saw the car drive up, so I went back and I said, "Mr. Justice"—he knew nothing about this, we'd kept it a secret—"I think President Roosevelt is calling." "Don't be an idiot, boy," he said, using a

1

favorite expression with his secretaries, "the president wouldn't call on me." I said, "Well, let me go back again." Then I told him it was the president. Then he said, "Give me a hand and help me change my coat." After he got his coat changed, I went downstairs and came up in the elevator with the president and Jimmy Roosevelt. Mrs. Roosevelt and Felix were on hand too. And, of course, the servants were looking out of doorways and around corners.

I heard very litle of the conversation. I remember that Holmes pointed to some swords over the fireplace and the president observed that they were handsome swords and Holmes said, "Yes. They were my Grandfather Jackson's who fought in the Indian Wars and that carries us back pretty well." And he said, "I remember my father's story of his father bringing home for lunch a friend he had met downtown in Boston that day and the friend said 'I saw that little West Indian bastard this morning,' meaning Alexander Hamilton."

Then F.D.R. said that his grandmother had told him that her father had fought in the Indian Wars too. Then as all were about to leave, the justice was asked by the president, "Well, can you give me any advice with your wisdom?" Holmes said, "Well, Mr. President, when your troops are in row and then you reorganize the regiments and battalions, you charge forward. I'd give the order to charge, just as you've done." Then the president said to the justice, "Thank you for your kind advice, but is there anything I can do for you?" There had been a bank holiday and the justice always paid his servants in cash and he had missed paying them in cash. He said "Yes, if you could just make an exception, not for all Supreme Court justices, just for retired justices, and let them get enough money to pay their servants in cash while the banks are closed, I'd appreciate it." Then they both laughed and the party moved on. Outside a crowd had gathered and the president, Felix and Jimmy got into the open car, while Mrs. Roosevelt walked back to the White House. Just before the car moved off, a loud voice shouted from the crowd, "Hey, Felix!" It was Thomas Reed Powell, Professor of Law at the Harvard Law School.[5]

It was a great occasion and a very touching thing for the president to do.

Afterward, the justice said that he had known the president when he was assistant secretary of the Navy during World War I, but that his face had changed. "He has a much stronger face than when I knew him before," he asserted. "He had a very

handsome face then, but there was a weakness in it. Now, there
is strength in it."

Wendell Holmes was a Bostonian to the manner born. His
first appearance at the "hub of the solar system," as his father
described it,[6] came on March 8, 1841. His physician father,
discoverer of the cause of puerperal fever, had become famous
at twenty-one by writing the poem "Ay! tear her tattered ensign
down"[7] to prevent the breaking-up of the *U.S.S. Constitution.*
Dr. Holmes, the descendant of Calvinist ministers of the Gospel was feisty and garrulous at five-foot-three. His wife, Amelia
Jackson, was as quiet and retiring as her husband was extro-
verted. Her father had been a noted Massachusetts legal figure
and a justice of the Supreme Judicial Court of the state.

The boy, called Wendell, thus began life with the advantages
of a closely knit family, social status, notable forebears and
economic security. Subsequently, his education included studies at the so-called Latin school of Epes Dixwell (his future
father-in-law) and four years at Harvard College. There he
gained some reputation for questioning accepted religious proprieties, learned to take his glass of wine, joined Alpha Delta
Phi and Porcellian, was cited for breaking windows,[8] and read
the Class Ode at Commencement on June 21, 1861—which he
attended after having enlisted as a private in the Massachusetts
Volunteer Militia.

Commissioned a first lieutenant in the twentieth Regiment,
Massachusetts Volunteers on July tenth, he and his fellows
were mustered into federal service and left for Washington in
September. From there he was moved quickly to confront the
enemy and was seriously wounded in the chest in his first
engagement on October twenty-first, when at Ball's Bluff on the
Potomac the Confederate forces caught the ill-advised Union
troops in a murderous trap as they sought to capture an impregnable position. After convalescing in Philadelphia and Boston
(with the benefit of the ministrations of a covey of devoted
women), he returned to combat.

In the remaining three years of his enlistment, he received
two more wounds. He was shot in the neck at Antietam—one of
the twenty-three thousand casualties of that day of carnage. In
the absence of minimal medical facilities, he was brought back

to Boston by Dr. Holmes. To Wendell's disgust, his father wrote
the dramatic details of his rescue in "My Search for the Captain," an article published in the *Atlantic Monthly*.[9] The story
provided the first components of the glamorous figure Wendell
was to become. After his second recovery, he returned to the
war in Virginia and was wounded in the heel by a piece of
shrapnel near Chancellorsville, at Marye's Heights. Saved from
a feared amputation, he was assigned to the Sixth Corps in time
to be rushed to Washington for the defense of that city against
Confederate General Early's encircling threat.

After sharing in the successful engagement at Fort Stevens,
he was discharged at the end of his three year enlistment
period, although the war was not over. He disregarded the
advice of his father, who thought the pursuit of the law narrow-
ing, and entered Harvard Law School. After finishing his
courses of study at the Law School and in private offices, he
was admitted to the Massachusetts Bar on March 4, 1867.
When he began practicing law in Boston, Wendell engaged in
the varied activities of the lawyer of that time, trying cases,
arguing appeals, and drawing documents. But it was soon obvious that he lacked the zest for mundane detail and the
forceful qualities required of a successful practitioner. Increasingly his interests lay in scholarly aspects of the law. In
this pursuit, in addition to his daily professional tasks, he acted
as editor and wrote for the *North American Review*. He also
revised and modernized Chancellor Kent's *Commentaries*, an
American legal classic and lectured at Harvard on American
history. These demanding academic activities were rewarding—
satisfying his speculative and intellectual nature.

After a certain amount of pressure from his Uncle John
Holmes, Wendell married Fanny Bowditch Dixwell on June 17,
1871. Fanny was the daughter of Wendell's former school
teacher and a descendant of John Dixwell, a signer of the death
warrant of Charles I. Fanny was also a granddaughter of
Nathaniel Bowditch, the author of the classic Bowditch's *Practical Navigator*. About the time he was married, Wendell embarked upon a project he later described to Brown University
graduates as a "start for the Pole." This was his preparation for
writing his *magnum opus* on the history and nature of the
common law which he hoped would bring him the fame his

ambitious nature craved. Thinking of himself as an explorer setting forth across the arctic ice in search of the North Pole, he faced "the loneliness of original work" in the field of legal scholarship.

He abandoned relaxation and diversion until the job was done. Fanny encouraged his rigorous schedule and loyally exhibited a steely resolve in sharing the attendant austerity. Living in rooms over a drug store at 10 Beacon Street, the couple were as one in the pursuit of the great objective and in March 1881, the year of Wendell's fortieth birthday,[10] they saw the publication of *The Common Law*[11]—one of the great legal works of all time. This treatise was calculated to bring him what he sought: a fame separate from his father's as well as appreciation of his worth from his peers. In one swoop, he invigorated the historical approach to the study of the law and he also changed the traditional view of the legal process by urging and using an examination based upon perceived reality rather than upon sterile tradition. He scorned the complex structures of Christopher Columbus Langdell, dean of the Harvard Law School, and other "legal theologians" and asserted the need for a concept of law that stressed the pragmatic and the useful.

Wendell's fame as a legal scholar spread widely and in early 1882 brought to him the invitation of Professor James Bradley Thayer of the Harvard Law School and of University President Charles W. Eliot to fill the specially founded Weld Professorship[12] in constitutional law. Wendell took the major step of abandoning the practice of law and accepted the generous offer. But after starting his duties at the law school in the fall, he made another major reversal of direction when in December he accepted an appointment to the Supreme Judicial Court of the State of Massachusetts and immediately left his teaching. Although Wendell had technically made provision for such an eventuality in his correspondence about the position, his abrupt departure was not well received by the authorities at Harvard; a marked coolness developed between him and Professors James Bradley Thayer and James Barr Ames.

Although no one then could have foreseen it, with this judicial appointment, Wendell began a career on the bench which would last fifty years. He served on the Massachusetts Court for twenty years—the last three as chief justice—and he served for nearly thirty years on the Supreme Court of the United States as Associate Justice.

BAY STATE JUSTICE

His twenty years on the state bench, marked Holmes as a jurist of learning, of ability, and of independent mind. His name was affixed to the large volume of opinions in rather ordinary tort and contract cases which engaged the courts in that period, but he also wrote a variety of opinions which set him above the ordinary and gave prominence to his judicial approach. In some cases, he revealed a conventional and conservative attitude, as when he supported a law which prohibited speeches on the Boston Common without a license from the mayor in one case[13] and in another sustained a regulation which authorized the firing of a policeman for taking part in political activity.[14]

In several other cases, however, he cut out from the pack and carved out striking and individualistic positions which departed from traditional norms and asserted expansive and liberal doctrines. He was judging at a time of industrial ferment. The emergence of large, powerful corporations had created a disproportionate influence on the side of the employers against the workers. For self-protection, workers were beginning to organize in unions to bargain on wages and working conditions. It was also a period when widespread mechanization and increasing complexity of equipment constantly threatened serious injury to "factory hands" in the plants. Massachusetts, with its large woolen mills and other major manufacturing enterprises, was a center of this conflict with workers' representatives pressing for and obtaining protective legislation while powerful opposing elements marshaled their forces to fight change.

Wendell was in the minority—usually of one—in these cases and for this reason spoke at first with some diffidence. Later, he wrote with increased force, but he was not able to carry his more traditional brethren with him.

Ryalls v. *Mechanics' Mills* (1889), 150 Mass. 190, dealt with injuries at work. A plaintiff worker had obtained a favorable verdict in the lower court for injuries caused by a defect in machinery. Wendell's appellate brethren reversed the verdict on the grounds that a statute recently passed required notice of injury which had not been given. Wendell cast his vote for the injured party, asserting that the statute did not intend to take away the worker's previous common law right to sue without notice.

Commonwealth v. *Perry* (1891), 155 Mass. 117, concerned punitive management practices against workers. Mill workers' representatives had obtained a law that forbade an employer to impose a fine or withhold wages for imperfections in cloth arising during weaving. Six justices held that the law was invalid because it violated the Massachusetts Constitution which protected the "inalienable right of acquiring, possessing and protecting property" including the "right to make reasonable contracts" of employment. Wendell, in lone dissent, held that the legislature could restrict employers in the punitive conditions they could impose on contracts of work and could legislate here as they had legislated to strike down contracts involving gaming and usury.

The McKinley Tariff Act of 1891 had set tariffs at record highs and had greatly increased the cost of living. Among the attempts to alleviate distress was a law that authorized a city to buy coal and wood to resell to its inhabitants. In *Opinion of the Justices in re: House Bill 519* (1892), 155 Mass. 598, a majority of the court held that maintaining a fuel yard was not a "public service"; it was an illegal exercise of public powers since private enterprise could perform this function. Wendell asserted that the activity should have been permitted since it was no less a public purpose than was supporting paupers, providing gas and electricity, furnishing education, and taking land for a railroad.

Vegelahn v. *Guntner* (1896), 167 Mass. 92, became Wendell's most publicized Massachusetts opinion. The majority of the court held that "patrolling or picketing" by union sympathizers outside an establishment that was on strike constituted unlawful interference with the rights of employer and employees to maintain the enterprise and to continue or obtain employment and could be enjoined. Wendell dissented. There was no threat of force involved, he wrote, and even though there might be consequent damage to the employer, some damage might be permissible if justified by considerations of policy and social advantage. With free competition, he asserted, combination is inevitable and where "combination on one side is patent and powerful, combination on the other is the necessary and desirable counterpart, if the battle is to be carried on in a fair and equal way." The proper objective, he maintained, would be for combined workers to have the same liberty as combined capital "to support their interests by agreement, persuasion, and the bestowal of those advantages which they otherwise control." Even though he was joined by Chief Justice Walbridge A. Field, Wendell's opinion fluttered a few dovecotes in the Bay State.

Wendell took a step further in another labor case where an employer was caught in the middle in a jurisdictional dispute between two unions. Wages were not the issue, but rather membership in one union or the other. The defendant union had lost members to the plaintiff union and now sought by threats of strikes and boycotts to induce the employer to pressure its employees to join or rejoin the defendant union; the plaintiff union sought an injunction. A majority of the court held the secondary boycott illegal. Wendell, on the other hand, held that the activity of the questing union was not illegal. He would have extended the doctrine of his *Vegelahn* dissent, since adopted as law, to this peripheral situation. In this case of *Plant* v. *Woods* (1900), 176 Mass 492, he asserted that "Unity of organization is necessary to make the contest of labor effectual." This was an advanced position on the rights of organized labor for those days and is, in fact, even for today. It was particularly significant in view of Wendell's opinion of the value of the strike as a tool of social progress. In the *Plant* case, he emphasized that he had no illusions as to the worth of the strike. "It is a lawful instrument in the universal struggle of life, . . . but is pure phantasy to suppose that there is a body of capital of which labor, as a whole, secures a larger share by that means." The organized, he added, simply got a larger share at the expense of the less-organized.

Wendell demonstrated from these cases that he was not a routine justice producing hackneyed law. He showed a sensitivity to opinions that were agitating the public. He gave heed, in his own words in *The Common Law*, to "the felt necessities of the time, the prevalent moral and political theories and intuitions of public policy, avowed or unconscious." In an economy oriented to the philosophy of private business, he struck a new note in finding possible limits to freedom of enterprise, broader areas for governmental regulation and acceptable functions for labor organizations. In this manner, he established the basic elements of a judicial philosophy which came to be considered as Holmesian.

His departures from the norm plus a willingness to speak in dissent caused some people to think of him as "a dangerous fellow,"[15] but his forthrightness, his tolerance of social experimentation, and his sensitivity to progressive trends of thought made him an outstanding figure among the judges of the nation. Accordingly, when Associate Justice Horace Gray, of Massachusetts, a member of the Supreme Court of the United States, died in 1902, Wendell's position plus his three years of service as chief justice of his state court made him an obvious candidate for the federal bench.

It was no incumbrance to Wendell's advancement that he had known Senator Henry Cabot Lodge since their younger days and the senator, strongly encouraged by Mrs. Lodge according to Wendell, sent his name to President Theodore Roosevelt for consideration. Roosevelt felt that Wendell conformed to the progressive image he was seeking to create for himself and the Republican party. He invited Wendell to Oyster Bay for a careful vetting and after a symbolic bending of the knee the president sent Wendell's name to the Senate for confirmation.

Senator George Frisbie Hoar, the senior senator from Massachusetts, reflecting the unhappiness of some of the community with Wendell's advanced stands, growled and grumbled and delayed, but eventually he surrendered and permitted the nomination to go on to Senate approval; Wendell was sworn in and took his seat on the highest court in the land on December 8, 1902.

ON THE HIGH COURT

Wendell's service on the Supreme Court of the United States is one of the great sagas of American law. Appointed at sixty-one he served until he was almost ninety-one, sitting through the administrations of six presidents. From the beginning, his opinions were noteworthy. They were couched in elegant and brilliant language, a rare phenomenon in legal writing. They also showed a freshness of approach and an independence of mind. In fact, in his first noted dissent in *Northern Securities Co.* v. *U.S.* (1904), 193 U.S. 197, argued in the year after his appointment, he voted in the minority against the trust-busting policy of the Roosevelt administration and thereby incurred the wrath of the president who had appointed him and had looked for more support in tightening the reins on big business.

Much of Wendell's popular fame rested upon a series of brilliantly expressed dissents from the ruling conservative majority of the Court. They covered a period of several decades and dealt with a variety of constitutional questions relating to the authority of legislatures to deal with the complex problems of modern industrial society. Shifting from the conservative position (espoused in the *Northern Securities Co.* case, where he had been motivated by his admiration for the empire-building titans of big business),[16] he adopted a hands-off attitude toward the exercise of legislative powers in cases dealing with the rights of labor and individual citizens.

Following the line of reasoning he had adopted in Massachusetts, in *Adair* v. *U.S.* (1907), 208 U.S. 161, Wendell dissented from the Court majority. He voted to uphold the provision of the Erdman Act that penalized employers for threatening job loss to employees who joined a union. This provision, the majority said, invaded rights of contract of employer and employee protected by the Fifth Amendment and was invalid. Wendell (with McKenna) disagreed. Congress might constitutionally decide, he asserted, that fostering strong union "was for the best interests, not only of the men, but of the railroads and the country at large." Wendell's dissenting view eventually became the law of the land, but it took many years to achieve this result.

In *Lochner* v. *New York* (1905), 198 U.S. 45, encouraging play in the legislative machinery, he voted against his brethren to uphold a statute which limited working hours for bakers to ten a day.

In the powerful language of his classic dissent, Wendell set forth his persuasive philosophy:

This case is decided upon a theory which a large part of the country does not entertain. If it were a question whether I agreed with that theory, I should desire to study it further and long before making up my mind. But I do not conceive that to be my duty, because I strongly believe that my agreement or disagreement has nothing to do with the right of a majority to embody their opinions in law. It is settled by various decisions of this court that state constitutions and state laws may regulate life in many ways which we as legislators might think injudicious or if you like as tyrannical as this, and which equally with this interfere with the liberty of contract. Sunday laws and usury laws are ancient examples. A more modern one is the prohibition of lotteries. The liberty of the citizen to do as he likes so long as he does not interfere with the liberty of others to do the same, which has been a shibboleth for some well-known writers, is interfered with by school laws, by the Post Office, by every state or municipal institution which takes his money for purposes thought desirable, whether he likes it or not. The Fourteenth Amendment does not enact Mr. Herbert Spencer's Social Statics. . . . Some of these laws embody convictions or prejudices which judges are likely to share. Some may not. But a constitution is not intended to embody a particular economic theory, whether of paternalism or of *laissez faire*. It is made for people of fundamentally differing views, and the accident of our finding certain opinions natural and familiar or novel and even shocking ought not to conclude our judgment upon the question whether statutes embodying them conflict with the Constitution of the United States.

Dissenting in *Truax* v. *Corrigan* (1921), 257 U.S. 312, he added:

There is nothing that I more deprecate than the use of the Fourteenth Amendment beyond the absolute compulsion of its words to prevent the making of social experiments that an important part of the community desires, in the insulated chambers afforded by the several States, even though the experiments may seem futile or even noxious to me. . . .

In *Coppage* v. *Kansas* (1915), 236 U.S. 1, along with Justices Day and Hughes, he plumped for broader powers and disagreed with the majority view that the Due Process clause of the Fourteenth Amendment invalidated a Kansas statute that made it a misdemeanor for an employer to require an employee to agree not to become a member of a union during his employment. He was "strongly of the opinion that there (was) nothing in the Constitution" to require the court to strike down the law. Citing his views in the *Vegelahn* and *Plant* cases in Massachusetts, he maintained that the *Adair* and *Lochner* cases should be overruled. The "constitutional freedom of contract" which they purported to protect he considered a fictitious and doctrinaire interpretation of the Constitution.

Child labor was a burning issue and an attempt to limit it resulted in *Hammer* v. *Dagenhart* (1917), 247 U.S. 251, where a bare majority of the Court (a five to four decision) held unconstitutional a federal statute that prohibited the transportation in commerce of goods produced by children under the age of fourteen. The manufacture of goods was not commerce and the federal government could not deal with it, the majority said: the fact that the goods were afterwards shipped in interstate commerce did not change the matter. Wendell, carrying Brandeis, Clarke, and McKenna with him, asserted that the constitutional power to regulate commerce "could not be cut down or qualified by the fact that it might interfere with the carrying out of the domestic policy of any State." If, however, policy were to be considered as the majority seemed to believe, then, said Wendell: ". . . if there is any matter upon which civilized countries have agreed—far more unanimously than they have with regard to intoxicants and some other matters over which this country is now aroused—it is the evil of premature and excessive child labor. I should have thought that if we were to introduce our own moral conceptions where in my opinion they do not belong, this was preëmently a case for upholding the exercise of all its powers by the United States."

Wendell's most memorable and most famous opinion is his dissent in *Abrams* v. *U.S.* (1919), 250 U.S. 616, which, as Felix Frankfurter said, "will live as long as English prose has the power to thrill."

The defendants had published two leaflets that opposed the sending of American troops into Russia after the Revolution of 1917, charging that capitalism was the enemy and advocating a general strike. They were charged under the Espionage Act, found guilty, and sentenced to twenty years in prison. Although Wendell had voted seven months earlier to uphold the conviction of Eugene V. Debs for attempting to obstruct wartime recruiting, in *Abrams,* after the war was over, he voted to reverse the convictions. . .

> It is only the present danger of immediate evil or the intent to bring it about that warrants Congress in setting a limit to the expression of opinion where private rights are not concerned. Congress certainly cannot forbid all effort to change the mind of the country. . .
>
> In this case sentences of twenty years imprisonment have been imposed for the publication of two leaflets that I believe the defendants had as much right to publish as the Government has to publish the Constitution of the United States now vainly invoked by them. Even if I am wrong and enough can be squeezed from these poor and puny anonymities to turn the color of legal litmus paper. . . the most nominal punishment seems to me all that possibly could be inflicted, unless the defendants are to be made to suffer not for what the indictment alleges but for the creed that they avow—a creed that I believe to be the creed of ignorance and immaturity when honestly held. . . .
>
> When men have realized that time has upset many fighting faiths, they may come to believe even more than they believe the very foundations of their own conduct that the ultimate good desired is better reached by free trade in ideas—that the best test of truth is the power of the thought to get itself accepted in the competition of the market. . . . That at any rate is the theory of our Constitution. It is an experiment, as all life is an experiment. Every year if not every day we have to wager our salvation upon some prophecy based upon imperfect knowledge. . . .

These were the "progressive" opinions upon which much of Wendell's contemporaneous *persona* was based. Still, he was not at all a convinced or knee-jerk liberal. This was attested to by his attitude toward the Sacco-Vanzetti case, in which his friend Frankfurter was deeply implicated in defense of the accused. Wendell, after their conviction and sentencing to death, refused twice to grant an application of *habeas corpus* on their behalf. This case was a left-wing *cause célèbre* all over the world. His was a skeptical, case-by-case approach. His skepticism was illustrated by a meeting, described by Francis Biddle, between Wendell and John W. Davis,[17] then solicitor general, in a corridor of the Capitol where the Court then sat.

"Mr. Solicitor General," asked Wendell, "how many more of those economic policy cases have you got?"

"Quite a basketful," Davis answered airily.

"Well, bring 'em on," said Wendell, "and we'll decide 'em. Of course, I know, and every sensible man knows, that the Sherman law[18] is damned nonsense, but if my country wants to go to hell, I am here to help it do it."

Not only did he vote to sustain convictions in several other free speech cases,[19] but he also took the conservative side in a variety of controversies which positioned him with the propertied interests, the titans and the moguls. In *Pennsylvania Coal Co.* v. *Mahon* (1922), 260 U.S. 393, the company owning land deeded the surface to grantees, reserving the right to remove all coal underneath. The removal caused subsidence and the legislature enacted a statute forbidding mining so as to cause subsidence of a habitation or a street. With John W. Davis, now a private practitioner, arguing the case for the company, Wendell, writing for the majority, held the law invalid as exceeding the police power and denying the company due process of law. To many, he seemed to be taking the position against which he had previously dissented. The case produced an unusual situation: Wendell wrote the majority opinion and Brandeis dissented. Usually they voted together. Professor Thomas Reed Powell, of the Harvard Law School, explained the apparent aberration by noting that the case was decided in the year that Wendell had his prostate operation.

State-enforced sterilization raised its head in *Buck* v. *Bell* (1927), 274 U.S. 200. Wendell wrote the opinion that upheld a Virginia statute that authorized the sterilization of the feeble-minded. The plaintiff, Carrie Buck, eighteen years old, was the daughter of a feeble-minded mother and the mother of an illegitimate feeble-minded child. "Three generations of imbeciles are enough," wrote Wendell over the dissent of Mr. Justice Butler.

Wendell could be detached and technical. In *United Zinc & Chemical Company* v. *Britt* (1922), 258 U.S. 268, he wrote the majority opinion which reversed a verdict and judgment for the plaintiff which had been affirmed by the Circuit Court of Appeals. In this case, trespassing children, eight and eleven years old respectively, had gone swimming in an unfenced excavation site that contained water poisoned by sulphuric acid. The children died as a result of their exposure to the chemical. Applying what the dissenters called the Massachusetts "Draconian doctrine" of attractive nuisance, Wendell held that, as trespassers the children did not make liable the corporate owner who did not know of their actual presence. Chief Justice Taft and Justices Clarke and Day dissented.

In *Bartels* v. *Iowa (1923),* 262 U.S. 404 and in similar cases brought on by anti-German feeling in World War I, the Court majority held that state laws prohibiting the public school teaching of any language other than English was unconstitutional in depriving teachers of the liberty guaranteed by the Fourteenth Amendment. Wendell in dissent felt that it was not unreasonable to require pupils to speak only English at school. The statute did not assume "the character of a merely arbitrary fiat," he said.

Wendell was almost disingenuous in *American Banana Company* v. *United Fruit Company* (1909), 213 U.S. 347. While not purporting to do so, he upheld the right of the powerful defendant monopoly in Costa Rica to crush a modest competitor. His opinion contained a tortured ascription of jurisdiction and a dubious selection of facts. In 1903 United Fruit was the uncontested lord of the land, according to the German consul in Costa Rica. The "government" was in the pocket of the monopoly and at its instigation, the plaintiff's land had been seized by Costa Rican troops. Wendell held that the fictitious state was a sovereign entity and that the Boston corporation could not be held responsible in the courts of the United States for actions in Costa Rica. Chief Justice Fuller went along with the opinion, but, with his approval sent a note back to Wendell. "Yes," he wrote, "but a very hard extension of the rules." Thus, Wendell was fallible and on occasion could, as other judges did, rely upon superficial externals rather than the basic facts of a case. His disregard of the persons involved and his application of a decorous mask to the real situation has been brilliantly and wittily described by Professor (now Judge) John T. Noonan, Jr., in his *Persons and Masks of the Law.*[20]

Over its whole corpus, Wendell's contribution to the law of the land is hard to pigeonhole. As Professor Burton has said, his was "a sardonic rather than a magnetic personality."[21] The tally is contradictory. He could on the one hand produce the broad Olympian generalities of the Abrams case, while, on the other, he could generate the almost-comic case of *Baltimore and Ohio Railroad* v. *Goodman* (1927), 275 U.S. 66, where he ruled that if the driver of a car, about to cross a railroad track, "cannot be sure otherwise whether a train is dangerously near he must stop and get out of his vehicle . . . if he relies upon not hearing the train or any signal and takes no further precaution he does so at his own risk." This opinion was written only two years after Wendell willy-nilly substituted an automobile for his horse-drawn victoria.

The fifty years since Wendell's death have seen a great oscillation in his perceived standing among the great judges of the United States. Initially, his reputation was high[22] and his dissents became guideposts for judges who supported modern legislative solutions for the unprecedented problems of a new day. His dissent in the *Adkins* (minimum wage for women) case was relied upon fifteen years later in *West Coast Hotel Co.* v. *Parrish* to support a reversal in Court policy, and in 1937, the Wagner Act decisions marked an espousal of the policy which he had enunciated in his dissent in the *Lochner* case. Although he had passed from the scene, Wendell was in the position of the thinker whom he once eulogized: Even after he was dead he had "men moving to the measure of his thought."

With the Depression, public pressure for legislative action increased and, with economic collapse and the advent of a new administration, the mid-thirties saw the logjam broken and the passage of a wave of remedial legislation. Aided by the conversion and switch of Justices Roberts and Hughes,[23] the Supreme Court now ratified measures that it would previously have held unconstitutional. Even though he was no longer present in body, Wendell's spirit hovered over the new marble palace of the Court where a novel tolerance of experimentation and a freedom from dogmatism made themselves felt as New Deal laws—when they were worthy—were given the green light. The receptivity to popular movements and the truly American openness to new methods of managing public affairs which he passed on to his successors constituted as great a legacy to his fellow Americans as the bequest of his residuary estate which he left to the United States of America.

The period of the inflation of Wendell's reputation was followed by a period of deflation. Critics found weakness in his "grab bag of epigrams," in his easy generalization advocating "freedom for the thought we hate" (Nazism?), and reliance for the discovery of ultimate truth on the give-and-take of a competitive market-place of ideas. In many ways, as has been said, he was a nineteenth-century judge—he lived more of his life in that century—and was a product of the times when his philosophy was first formed. His concept of a harsh, positivist universe, his lack of interest in the "common man," his admiration for the free-wheeling giants of big business, his glorification of the soldier, his stress on force as the *ultima ratio* in human affairs and his skepticism about the beneficial effects of social legislation—and what he called "the upward and onward"—were not sympathetic views for more modern thinkers and caused many observers to lower his position in the legal Pantheon.

Contributing to this decline were a series of attacks begun by Jesuit lawyers and theologians six years after Wendell's death and continued with supplementary forays by lay critics for a period of some ten years.[24] These commentators found fault with Wendell's irreverence, his agnosticism, the relativity of his moral concepts, his dismissal of natural law, his positivism and his legal realism. He was even compared to Hitler by one vituperative analyst. Supporters promptly sprang to their guns and laid down a defensive fire.[25] Yale and Harvard responded to Georgetown and Fordham. Wendell's patriotism, his military service of his country, his respect for law, his youthful antislavery activism and the great opinions supporting free speech and the rights of labor and sustaining the actions of popular legislative bodies were stressed in his defense. Professor Paul Freund, of the Harvard Law School, although he found "limitations" in Wendell's empirical philosophical formulae, pointed out that Wendell was "writing in polemical context" in some instances and that "his rhetoric was designed to shock." He also characterized as "lacking in humor no less than in perception" those who associated Wendell with a totalitarian outlook—in view of his devotion to the free market in ideas and his even-handed administration of justice. Later historians have also found droll the lack of awareness of Wendell's ecclesiastical critics of the relativity of some of the doctrines and practices of their church then passionately held. Regrettably, Wendell was no longer in a position to enjoy the fun.

The controversy did not succeed in driving Wendell from a

foremost place in the legal Valhalla, but it did serve to make the elements of his greatness more realistic. More respectful, but less emotional appraisals over the years placed him in a significant, but less elevated, position. Professor Lon Fuller deprecated his lack of moral criteria. Yosal Rugat criticized his chosen role of "detached spectator" and his lack of commitment to "public responsibilities." The Holmes Lectures of 1981 at the Harvard Law School by Benjamin Kaplan, Patrick Atiyah, and Jan Vetter gently set him in a less exalted position among the great.[26] In the general shaking-down which history has provided, it is apparent that he was not quite the Grand Panjandrum (a description he liked)[27] he had once been considered. None of this affected the considered and glowing tribute of one eminent American authority. Writing to Michael Janeway, then a Harvard student, on May 24, 1960, and advising him "not to be disturbed by all the Jesuits have said about this most critical and articulate of agnostics," Dean Acheson said:

> One of the slipperiest words I know is "great." But I think the "greatest" man I have ever known, that is, the essence of man living, man thinking, man baring himself to the lonely emptiness—or the reverse—of the universe, was Holmes. Brandeis was eminent, but not his equal. George Marshall was a peer and in some ways—in transfiguration through duty, for instance—their superior. But there the class closes. Even the most intense devotion cannot open it further.[28]

A brilliant recent study of Wendell by one eminently qualified to judge concludes with as balanced an appraisal as we are likely to get:

> An interesting man, an interesting genius, with a heavy dose of elusiveness and self-contradiction. It would be condescension on our part to deny him his frailties while praising his strengths. His vision of law and legal process, as described in *The Common Law,* we have all appropriated and absorbed. We could not escape it if we would: it informs all we do as lawyers. We move to the measure of his thought.[29]

NOTES ON WENDELL

[1] Donald Hiss—Harvard Law graduate 1932, secretary to Wendell 1932–33, Washington lawyer, partner at Covington & Burling, younger brother of Alger Hiss.

[2] Thomas Gardiner Corcoran (1900–1981), graduate of Brown and Harvard Law School, secretary of Wendell in 1926–27, with Benjamin Cohen the drafter of many of the major New Deal laws, intimate of FDR whom he often entertained by singing and playing his accordian, later lobbyist and Washington insider of fabulous energy, dubbed "Tommy the Cork" by FDR.

[3] Felix Frankfurter (1882–1965), controversial Vienna-born teacher of law and polemicist, Byrne Professor of Administrative Law at Harvard Law School 1920–1939, intimate adviser to FDR, clandestine agent of Justice Brandeis, associate justice of the Supreme Court of the United States 1939–1962.

[4] Marvin McIntyre—newspaperman, expert in public relations and press secretary to FDR.

[5] Thomas Reed (Nuncie) Powell (1880–1955), professor of law at Columbia and Harvard. Sardonic and pungent commentator on Constitutional Law and the doings of the Supreme Court.

[6] This was the Boston State House. See Oliver Wendell Holmes, *Autocrat of the Breakfast Table* (Boston: Houghton, Mifflin and Company, 1891), ch. VI, p. 125.

[7] *Poetical Works of Oliver Wendell Holmes* (Boston: Houghton, Mifflin and Company, 1880), p. 1.

[8] Mark DeWolfe Howe, *Justice Holmes: The Shaping Years* (Cambridge: Harvard University Press, Belknap Press, 1957), p. 68.

[9] Oliver Wendell Holmes, "My Search for the Captain," *Atlantic Monthly*, December 1862.

[10] ". . . I hurried to get it out before March 8, because then I should be 40 and it was said that if a man was to do anything, he must do it before 40." Howe, *The Proving Years*, p. 135.

[11] Oliver Wendell Holmes, Jr., *The Common Law* (Little, Brown and Company, 1881).

[12] The chair had been established especially for Wendell through the contribution of William F. Weld, Jr., who had inherited three million dollars. Louis D. Brandeis helped to raise the money. Howe, *The Proving Years*, p. 264.

[13] *Commonwealth* v. *Davis* (1895), 162 Mass. 510.

[14] *McAuliffe* v. *New Bedford* (1892), 155 Mas. 216. "The plaintiff may have a constitutional right to talk politics, but he has no constitutional right to be a policeman. . . ."

[15] Holmes to Pollock, August 13, 1902: "There have been powerful interests against me, because some at least of the money powers think me dangerous, wherein they are wrong." Howe, *Holmes-Pollock Letters*, vol. 1, p. 103.

[16] Wendell was particularly impressed by the aggressive activities of James J. Hill, the railroad magnate, and others whose energies did much to turn the wheels of the economic machine. "Hill," Wendell told Pollock, had "an immense mastery of economic details, and equal grasp of general principles, and ability and courage to put his conclusions into effect when all the knowing ones said he would fail." *Holmes-Pollock Letters*, vol. 1, p. 167.

[17] John William Davis (1873–1955), famous American constitutional lawyer and unsuccessful candidate for the presidency against Coolidge in 1924. He argued 140 cases before the Supreme Court of the United States. A native of West Virginia, he served in the U.S. House of Representatives (1911–13). He was also ambassador to Great Britain (1918–21).

[18] The Sherman Anti-Trust Act of 1890 prohibited illegal combinations in the form of business trusts. It was reinforced by the Clayton Act in 1914 and other later legislation.

[19] *Schenck* v. *U.S.* (1919), 249 U.S. 47. *Debs* v. *U.S.* (1919), 249 U.S. 211.

[20] John T. Noonan, Jr., *Persons and Masks of the Law* (New York: Farrar, Straus and Giroux, 1976), p. 65.

21 David H. Burton, *Oliver Wendell Holmes* (Boston: Twayne Publishers, 1980), p. 144.

22 Although his reputation was high, even at Harvard there were reservations. As early as 1934, Professor Edward H. (Bull) Warren, when asked about the status of Wendell as a judge, after a long pause and a rolling of the eyes, placed him in "the first hundred" of American judges.

23 They were struck by the white light on the road to Damascus, according to Professor Thomas Reed Powell, of the Harvard Law School.

24 Francis E. Lucey, "Jurisprudence and the Future Social Order" *Social Science*, 16:211–217 (July 1941). Ben W. Palmer, "Hobbes, Holmes and Hitler," *American Bar Association Journal*, 31:569 (1945).

25 Mark DeWolfe Howe, "The Positivism of Mr. Justice Holmes" *Harvard Law Review*, 64:529 (1951). On this matter generally, see: E. Purcell, "The Crisis of Democratic Theory," 159–78 (1973). David H. Burton, "Justice Holmes and the Jesuits," *The American Journal of Jurisprudence*, 27:32 (1983).

26 Lon Fuller, *The Law in Quest of Itself* (1940).
Yosal Rugat, "The Judge as Spectator," *31 University of Chicago Law Review, 213* (1964).
Benjamin Kaplan, Patrick Atiyah and Jan Vetter, *Holmes and The Common Law: A Century Later—The Holmes Lectures, 1981*. Occasional Pamphlet Number Ten (Harvard Law School, Cambridge, Massachusetts, 1983).
For a pungent revisionist opinion see also: H.L. Mencken, "Mr. Justice Holmes," *American Mercury*, May 1930 and May 1932 in ed. Alistair Cooke, *The Vintage Mencken* (New York: Vintage Books, 1955).

27 Grand Panjamdrum describes a "powerful personage" and was a burlesque title invented by Samuel Foote (1720–1777).
Webster, *New International Dictionary*, 1949, p. 1764.

28 David C. Acheson and David S. McLean, eds., *Among Friends: Personal Letters of Dean Acheson*, May 24, 1960 (N.Y.: Dodd, Mead, 1980), pp. 182–183.

29 Benjamin Kaplan, "Encounters With O. W. Holmes, Jr.," *Harvard Law Review*, 1828, 1852, (1983) appropriating a portion of a sentence of Wendell:
"the secret isolated joy of the thinker who knows that, a hundred years after he is dead and forgotten, men who never heard of him will be moving to the measure of his thought."

The Persona

This was Oliver Wendell Holmes, Jr., the Olympian historical figure. What of Wendell Holmes, the person? What was he
like at close quarters? How did he look? How did he act? How
did he sound? Did he have foibles? What was his personal
myth?

Fortunately, it was possible to find and interview people who
knew Wendell and could testify to his unique and appealing
human qualities. They included the head of his household after
Fanny Holmes's death, seven of his former secretaries, two
women who, as young brides, listened to his conversation,
shared his automobile rides, and helped him fight boredom; a
family friend who was the wife of one of his secretaries; and a
young couple who were guests in his household. Their recollections and judgments provide an invaluable fund of information.
They show him to have been tolerant and arrogant, conservative and liberal, earthy and ethereal, warm and coolly
intellectual, patriotic, vain, witty and loyal. In short: a human
being.

STYLE AND ACCOUTERMENT

An appraisal of Wendell must begin with his superb physical
endowment. In his prime, he stood about six-foot-two. With his
ruddy complexion, full head of white hair, sweeping cavalry
mustache, and courtly manner, he made an immediate and
striking impression. A photo of him[1] in an English garden—
taken by his friend, Sir Leslie Scott, in 1909 when Wendell
received an honorary degree of Doctor of Civil Laws at Oxford—shows the full aura of his maturity and reproduces the
characteristic gleam in his eye which betokens his zest and
health. With this photo as evidence, it is easy to credit the quote
attributed by Harold Laski to Lady Oxford[2] who: ". . . was
talking of eyes and said that in the 90s you had a provocative

21

gleam that might easily have tempted her had occasion offered; and old Lady Horner[3] was of the same opinion."[4]

Alger Hiss,[5] Wendell's secretary in 1929–30, vividly recalls his first impression of Wendell:

> When I met him for the first time in 1929, he looked very much like the Hopkinson portrait of him at the Harvard Law School, which was painted at that time. His appearance was stunning, regal almost, and he was very erect in spite of his eighty-eight years. He dressed with careful taste and was proud of his appearance. His voice was vigorous and his enunciation was clear. His choice of words was extraordinary. He spoke with what I would call a first-class Middle Atlantic accent, not as markedly patrician as Franklin Roosevelt's nor an accent which struck the ear and which you were conscious of.

Professor W. Barton Leach,[6] Wendell's secretary in 1924–25, also remembered the Hopkinson portrait and was intrigued with some differences between the study and the real Holmes:

> I wish I liked the Hopkinson[7] portrait. . . . It is a splendid portrait by an able artist. But, as I look at it, I always expect the old man to stick his head out from behind the frame with a sly smile on his face and wink. As a matter of fact, this practically happened. I saw the portrait first at Beverly Farms when the head had been finished and the robes had been sketched in charcoal on the canvas. As we walked into the room—he and I and his then secretary, John Lockwood[8]—and I got my first look at the portrait. . . . I stood back, cocking my head to one side as if I knew something about art, and said "oh" and "ah" at intervals which seemed to me to be appropriate—for I knew one of the justice's most deep-seated (and appealing) qualities was a good, wholehearted, ingenuous vanity, particularly concerning his personal appearance. The justice also looked long at the painting with the expression of one who is participating in the perpetration of a harmless practical joke, and said, "Rather an imposing old bugger, isn't he!" I made a banal remark designed to indicate concurrence with the adjective, but dissent from the noun. He added, "That isn't me, but it's a damn good thing for people to think it is."

Augustin Derby,[9] Wendell's secretary in 1906–07, had an earlier opportunity to observe Wendell and a later chance to note the changes effected by time:

Early in 1906, I called upon him at his home, 1720 I [Eye] Street, in Washington. My first impression of him is still vivid; erect and lean, a mass of gray hair, and gray military mustache, keen piercing, but very kindly eyes, as handsome a man as I have ever known. Gutzon Borglum,[10] the well-known sculptor who took Wendell's death mask, is reported in the press to have said that the features were as fine as any he had ever seen in Greek, Roman or Anglo-Saxon sculpture.

Late in March, 1934, I called at his home. . . . I found the justice sitting in a familiar rocking chair smoking a cigar. He seemed more bent than the last time I had seen him (he had passed his ninety-third birthday), his voice was not so vibrant, but he had that same look of great distinction.

Donald Hiss, Wendell's secretary in 1932–33, had a slightly different memory:

"He was just a magnificent-looking person. Beautiful white hair and mustache, ruddy cheeks and piercing blue eyes— lovely eyes that could glare at you if you mispronounced a word, which I frequently did, reading to him."

The resonant baritone voice which Wendell used so effectively left a lasting impression. One woman[11] who had visited him at I Street later said: "I don't recall the occasions for our visits or what we talked about, but *that voice* . . . I'll never forget that voice."

A secretary described his attire: "He dressed with careful taste and was proud of his appearance. In those days, everyone on the Court wore a cutaway with his gown over it and the lawyers had to wear them as well. He got most of his clothes from a London tailor and that was a mark—in the nineteenth and early twentieth centuries—of a gentleman's taste that didn't require further proof."

Donald Hiss added further details: "Sometimes he would wear a regular business suit, but usually he wore striped trousers. Then he had an old alpaca coat that he used to wear to walk around in and sit around in, but when he would go out, he would put his regular coat on."

Some of those who knew the justice retained less relaxed memories. Katharine L. Bundy,[12] who met Wendell when she was the fiancée of one of the secretaries, spoke of the awe she felt in Wendell's company: "I was as scared of him as you could be. Twice a summer, I would call on him—which would scare me to death. I never got over being scared."

HEALTH AND VIGOR

In view of the rudimentary medical care of that day, Wendell's survival of the Civil War—having been wounded three times—amply proved the strength of his constitution. For three years he endured close, bloody, and constant fighting.[13] He slept on the ground in all weathers, ate execrable food, contracted attendant diseases, and, above all, sustained the continual and shocking loss of intimate friends and fellow soldiers. Yet he came through the ordeal without permanent impairment because of a unique combination of physical and emotional resilience.

Wendell accepted this superb gift of the cosmos with appreciation. Until his very old age, except for irritating colds, an occasional twinge from his war wounds in bad weather, and a case of shingles, he enjoyed remarkable health. He successfully underwent a prostate removal when he was eighty-one and survived a heart attack eight years later. Yet, except for his regular daily walks, a brief experiment with bicycling, and a burst of mountain climbing in his youth, he never showed any interest in athletic activity, nor did he participate in games or follow the fortunes of collegiate or professional athletic teams.

"Golf! I should say not." he wrote to Lewis Einstein[14] in 1927. "I play no games that require intelligence (Bridge) or skill. Solitaire (my own rules) and a short toddle are enough for me now."[15]

A notable vigor flowed from this physical well-being.

A secretary, Alger Hiss, provides an example of this *joie de vivre:*

Professor Austin Scott,[16] of the Harvard Law School, has told of a visit he and Professor Sayre Macneil[17] made to the I Street house. At this time Holmes was in his seventies and it shows how vigorous he was. When they got to the house, they sent in their cards and, shortly thereafter, the judge came tripping down the stairs from the second floor. Typical of Holmes—he held up the cards and said, "First you shuffle / Then you deal / Which is Scott / And which Macneil?" Scott never forgot this. It was his introduction to Justice Holmes.

I recall another delightful demonstration of his vigor. When I was with Holmes at his summer home at Beverly Farms in 1930, Sir Frederick Pollock[18] and Lady Pollock came to visit him, and my wife and I were invited to attend a dinner he gave for them. Both Sir Frederick and Lady Pollock were rather frail. Holmes was then eighty-nine. Pollock was four years younger and his wife was about the same age, so that each of the elderly people was older than the combined ages of my wife and myself who were in our mid-twenties. The setting for the dinner was magnificent, with gleaming candlelight and all the crystal out; the gentlemen in black ties and the ladies in evening gowns. The meal was delicious and excellently served by Mary Donnellan.[19] In the course of the conversation, Lady Pollock referred to some common friend and Holmes asked how she was. Lady Pollock said, "Well, she's not doing so well. You know she's feeling her years." Holmes said, "Really? How old is she?" Lady Pollock said, "She must be eighty-four or eighty-five." And Holmes, with this beautiful baritone voice, the light shining on his white hair and mustache, from the head of the table where he was sitting, boomed out, "Why what's eighty among adults?"

This love of life persisted until his last years. Even though his view of the universe might not have been benevolent, he enjoyed being a part of it. When Wendell was ninety-two and physically declining, Mark Howe,[20] his then secretary, discussed the traditional Thanksgiving observance with him. Howe remembered, "When I said that it was somewhat absurd every year no matter what happened to compel everyone in the nation to give thanks, Holmes rather doubted the absurdity . . . saying we can always be thankful we are alive. This in perfect seriousness."

FOOD AND DRINK

Wendell greatly enjoyed the pleasures of the table and his metabolism allowed him to savor the delights of good food and wine long beyond the normal span of years. When he was young, his consumption of the latter was not always judicious. He told one secretary of a celebration in Cambridge at the Porcellian Club or at Alpha Delta Phi.[21] When he left in a tipsy condition, he went to the family home on Beacon Street. He got

as far as the vestibule where he spent the remainder of the night
and was found in the morning. His parents reacted in typical
but opposite fashion: His father was voluble and caustic for
weeks, but his mother never said a word—and that cut Wendell
to the quick.

His eating habits were described by another intimate: "He
attacked food with zest. He had a tremendous appetite and ate
massive breakfasts with porridge and cream, eggs, muffins,
marmalade and coffee. He would put enormous amounts of
anchovy paste under a poached egg. It would be enough to take
the head off an ordinary person." The anchovy paste was from
S. S. Pierce, the Boston grocer, and one day Wendell said to
Donald Hiss, "Do you think that they go onto the ocean and
ask if this is one of S. S. Pierce's anchovies before they grab
him?"

The description of Wendell's collations continued: "He said
that if all the cattle and sheep he had eaten in his life were put
into box cars, it would make an awfully long train. And he
loved 'the bubbly.' Whenever anyone presented him with
champagne during Prohibition, he would meet the ethical problem of judicial consumption by saying, 'I take judicial notice
that this is 'Pre-Prohibition!' " Barton Leach remembered another instance of Wendell's judicial gloss during Prohibition:
"Henry White sent three bottles of liquor to the Judge. He was
perplexed. 'The 18th Amendment forbids manufacture, transportation and importation. It does not forbid possession or use.
If I send it back, I'll be guilty of transportation. On the whole, I
think I shall apply the maxim *de minimis* and drink it.' "

Even when his metabolism no longer operated as it had in
his younger days, Wendell remained philosophical. Barton
Leach provided the following as one of Wendell's "maxims": "I
have God to thank for a rational constitution. When I was
young and could absorb liquor, I loved it. Now that I am old
and can't stand it, I really don't care for it." Leach also remembered him saying, "Contentment in life is nothing more than the
exertion to the limit of the powers God gave you." But as Leach
observed, "since advancing years put some obvious restric-
tions on the exertion of the powers referred to, several times I
heard him say, 'One of my greatest problems is to find available
vices for old age.' "

HOST AND GUEST

The author Owen Wister, as a young man in his twenties, received an impression of Wendell which remained vivid after fifty years. As a host in his cottage at Mattapoiset on Buzzard's Bay, Massachusetts about 1880, Wendell was

> . . . slim as a race horse when I first knew him; and had just finished making a cup with red wine for his three guests, informally asked to supper on the South Shore. The ice tinkled in the pitcher as he brought it in. Art had gone into this, as in all else that he does. Throughout the evening, it was my part to be seen and not heard for I was the youngest there. Two brilliant listeners—handsome ladies both—set his talk going; and I was captured by it then, as I have been captured by it since, through fifty years, often when he had no better listener than I. His talk would always bubble and sparkle from him in a stream of seriousness and laughter, imagination and philosophy, in which enthusiasm was undying; and the style of a master marked his improvisations, just as it marked his considered writing.[22]

In their early days in Washington, Wendell and Fanny were frequent diners-out and themselves entertained at I Street with formal dinners attended by people like the French ambassador, Jules Jusserand,[23] General and Mrs. Leonard Wood,[24] commander of the Rough Riders in the Spanish War, and Senator and Mrs. Henry Cabot Lodge,[25] all noted on Fanny's old place charts. Sunday evenings, the couple followed an established custom and took supper away from home at what Wendell called a "pothouse," often the old Powhatan at Eighteenth and Pennsylvania, just around the corner from their house.

A picture of Wendell as a dinner guest is set down in a fascinating diary by Ellen Maury Slayden,[26] the wife of a Texas member of Congress, whose sharp eye and caustic tongue rivalled those of Fanny:

> "The bells of hell go ting-a-ling
> For you, but not for me,
> The Angel choirs they sing-a-ling
> That's the goods for me.
> Oh, death where is thy sting-a-ling
> Where grave thy victoree?

When the bells of hell go ting-a-ling
For you but not for me?"

At a dinner at the Solicitor General's,[27] Justice Holmes repeated those lines in response to a plea of, "Do, Mr. Justice. Do give us your favorite poem." . . . At the dinner, Justice Holmes sat to Mrs. Davis' right, and I next to him. He is extraordinarily handsome, clear cut, humorous, and given to profanity in the old-fashioned aristocratic way that is never cheap or offensive. . . . When a certain Mr. Secretary came back from the smoking room, he explained that he had "asked the Justice's permission to leave ahead of him." Later I heard the Justice express himself forcefully about people who put rules of etiquette before common sense. He told me that William Jennings Bryan did not exist for him intellectually. He had built theories of government on phrases, not phrases on theories. Bill James, he said, asked him why he didn't join the Society for Psychical Research, and he retorted, "Why don't you investigate the religion of Mohammed?[28] Thousands are ready to die for it, and yet you might go to its depth and care no more for it than when you began, and that is the way I feel about psychical matters.' He declared that he wouldn't read a book written as much as twenty-five years ago. His infinite jest is refreshing after the owlish solemnity of smaller men.[29]

Ellen Slayden's vignette is a perfect picture of Wendell in full oratorical flight before a receptive audience. He does appear a bit cavalier in his dismissal of the one-time "Boy Orator of the Platte," but perhaps he had been influenced by the order of teetotaller Bryan's friend, Josephus Daniels, the secretary of the navy, that limited liquid consumption to grape juice in the wardrooms of the United States Navy.

EARTHINESS

Although the profanity to which Mrs. Slayden referred probably consisted only of a "damn" or "hell" here and there, Wendell had fought in infantry combat and knew all the words. On occasion he also seemed to enjoy using the most exotic form of profanity, as John Knox,[30] a young prelaw student from Chicago, discovered when he visited Wendell at Beverly Farms on a hot day in September 1930. As they were seated talking generalities, Knox "noticed that Holmes' vocabulary was becoming more and more interesting. His language began to be interspersed with many cuss words which he had evidently 'picked up' in the Civil War. I then decided to attempt to switch the topic of conversation to his war experiences as soon as I had the opportunity to do so. Without warning, however, he suddenly lapsed back into 'proper Bostonian English.' "

There was more than a trace of ham in Wendell. He loved to strike a dramatic pose. Combined with this tendency was a strong urge *épater le bourgeóis*. The combination of these qualities made a potent and dangerous mixture.

The youthful Erwin N. Griswold, later dean of the Harvard Law School, was given a glimpse of Wendell's theatrics when he visited at 1720 I Street in the spring of 1930. "As we went into his back room," Griswold later recalled, "he took a great big thick brief and threw it in the waste basket (I always assumed that the law clerk would be asked to take it out later). He said '147 pages long. I don't read 'em when they're that long and I don't care who knows it either. . . . I don't see why they don't suggest something and leave it to our imagination like a questionable French novel.' "

He loved shocking the complacent, and sometimes his words exceeded his meaning and horrified those of more pedestrian or less skeptical frames of mind. Such flippancy in describing the human condition and in describing the law itself stirred the Jesuits into action in the forties.

Wendell sampled the *épice* of Paris on one European trip by visiting the *Folies Bergéres* on an evening when Fanny was indisposed.[31] In those days, these *divertissements* were spicy, but not out of bounds for family entertainment. The redoubtable Katharine Bundy once pointed out that she took her three boys to the *Folies Bergéres,* as her father had first taken her when she was twenty (after they had first paused to buy a wedding band for her finger for propriety's sake). She further reported that her son, Mac, then twelve, "became terribly bored" and, perhaps in token of future seriousness, left the theatre to read a Rover Boys book "under a palm tree."

In Washington somewhat later, Wendell sought amusement in his regular trips to the Gayety burlesque theatre on Ninth Street, N.W. This was somewhat stronger fare than the old *Folies*. Under the management of the notorious Jimmy Lake, the old satire and vaudeville had given way to the *double entendre* and the strip tease. As Lake wrote in his book, *Footlights, Fistfights and Femmes,*[32] "When stripping became the vogue, I accepted it whole hog and gave my customers their money's worth."

When Wendell settled into his seat at the theatre, according to a secretary, he would turn to his neighbor in the audience and, appropriating a favorite comment of a western Massachusetts trial lawyer, say "Thank God, I've got low tastes!" Lake described Wendell's visits: "When the highly esteemed Justice Oliver Wendell Holmes put in his weekly appearance at the old burlesque house, he made this stock observation: 'Is it good and dirty this week? If not, I'm not going to stay.'"

Wendell's oft-repeated first principle which stressed the importance of keeping the bowels open is widely known, yet he had reservations about the desirability of explicating on the printed page the "physiology of copulation." In 1929, Wendell read Hemingway's *The Sun Also Rises* at the instigation of Owen Wister. Then Wendell wrote to his friend about the author and the book Wister had predicted would survive: "So let him survive—but as you prophesized he would, let him leave his garbage.

Wendell continued:

> It is singular. An account of eating and drinking with a lot of fornication accompanied by conversations on the lowest level, with some slight intelligence, but no ideas and nothing else— and yet it seems a slice of life, and you are not bored with the details of an ordinary day.
>
>   It reminds me of a reflection that I often make on how large a part of the time and thoughts of even the best of us are taken up by the animal wants.[33]

As Mark Howe put it: "He shows a peculiar sensitiveness to any unpleasant or degenerate implications in novels . . . as in *Three Cities*[34] the scene of the maid and the boyfriend. At the same time, he has a refreshing way of suddenly saying, in reading *Three Cities,* 'Am I to understand that the young man fucked his mother-in-law?'"[35]

Barton Leach remembered Wendell pointing out the phallic implications of one view of the telescope held at waist level by Admiral Farragut on the statue in the square near Wendell's house. In the course of the walks that Holmes and the young secretary took together, Wendell's observations were not always confined to the statuary. If they met women, "the Judge would look them all over up and down and if they were young and beautiful he would comment with the appreciation of a connoisseur upon the particular feature of beauty, whatever it was, all the way from the ankles to the hair."[36]

His delicacy about the sexual explicitness of modern literature did not prevent him from enjoying the raciness of Rabelais and the amorous adventures of Casanova to whom he resorted happily after finishing *The Common Law*. Among the moderns, he confessed to Pollock that Colette Willy's *Claudine en Ménage* had fascinated him, even though, as he said, it "describes unspeakable practices on the part of the heroine." He added, "One's jaw drops with amazement to find it assumed that two women can't be alone in a room together without exciting sinister suspicions."

He could describe a legal process with an excretive figure of speech, described by Mark Howe as a "typical Holmes conceit":

> He said that he was once in the lavatory in the Boston Court House and talked to the lawyer who was next to him who didn't seem to be too impressed by the simile, but Holmes always thought it a good one. That is that solving some problem in law is a good deal like pissing. When you piss, you don't do as you do when you move a finger—look at it, will its motion and understand its moving. You simply exert a pressure generally you don't know where—and you piss. To do it is as with reaching many solutions—you exert a dim pressure—you don't quite know where—and the solution appears.[37]

Some of the anecdotes about Wendell, while ringing true, are impossible to authenticate. One famous anecdote pictures Wendell and Brandeis leaving the Capitol together and having an attractive young blonde mince across their path. Wendell, then ninety, is reputed to have paused, sighed and said to Brandeis, "Oh, to be seventy again!"

Howe records one gurgle as from the cooling lava of a subsiding volcano, emitted when Wendell was ninety-two: "His cousin's daughter, recently married, whom he doesn't like, was expected for a call on him this morning. When she was announced by Mary as being downstairs, he simply said, "Jesus!"

THE MÉNAGE

When Wendell and Fanny were married, they lived very simply on the modest income earned from his law practice and his production of scholarly legal writings. Their first home was with his parents at 296 Beacon Street; in 1875 they moved to "rooms" above a drug store at 10 Beacon Street. These were Spartan beginnings, although the ambience of the latter was sufficiently acceptable for the young couple to entertain Oscar Wilde who "told them stories" one evening when he was on an American tour.

As their income increased, however, through judicial appointments and inheritance, their quarters rose in the scale. They moved to a lovely brick-fronted house at 9 Orchard Street on Beacon Hill. Then they had sole tenancy of the parental home on Beacon Street. Finally, they occupied the famous 1720 I Street in Washington.

With this rise in status came a corresponding growth in the size of the Holmes household. In their later years, it assumed what today would be considered baronial proportions. In the Washington house in the later twenties, the staff consisted of a cook, a kitchen maid, a maid, an upstairs maid, and a coachman who later became a chauffeur.[38] According to James H. Rowe,[39] the last in the long line of Holmes secretaries, the chauffeur was designated as an independent contractor rather than an employee because Wendell thereby proposed to insulate himself from an employer's liability for the negligent operation of the vehicle by a servant.

Beside this group, Wendell had a messenger for court activities and a "secretary" selected annually from the graduating class of the Harvard Law School. The star of the Holmes establishment was a young Irish woman named Annie Mary Donnellan, who became known as "Mary" because there was already an Annie Gough in the kitchen when she began work. Mary played a crucial role in the house after the death of Fanny.

Wendell was amply able to support the cost of this household. After the scrimping of their earliest years, he and Fanny had no worries about financial security.[40] After January 1, 1927, the pay of an associate justice of the Supreme Court was $20,000 a year, which would amount to $126,000 in 1986 dollars. When he died in 1935, his gross estate totalled $568,000 and even though this sum included real estate, his personal estate exceeded a half million dollars, which would be translated into 4.5 million in today's terms.[41] Having this capital in mind, it is fair to assume the Holmeses had an investment income of from $20,000 to $25,000 a year, making a total income of at least $40,000 a year or $300,000 at present values.[42] In assessing the value of income, we must remember that costs were much lower fifty years ago. The salary of Mary Donnellan, as maid, was seventy dollars a month with room and board. Income was tax free until 1913 and then was subject only to a modest federal tax ranging from 1 percent of $20,000 to 7 percent of income over a million. Thus, Wendell and Fanny were in a very special class so far as income was concerned. Although Wendell said in a famous quote: "Taxes are what we pay for civilized society," in fact there was no tax on income when he wrote those striking lines in the *Compañía de Tabácos*[43] case in 1904. One wonders if he would feel the same philosophical detachment under today's rates. Perhaps his capital would be invested in tax-exempt municipals.

Their failure to have children also placed Wendell and Fanny's household in a special category; they were spared the cares and diversions of couples who produce offspring. There has been great speculation as to the reason for this childlessness and certain statements of Wendell imply that this lack was due to a conscious decision.[44] But expressions of regret by Fanny plus the unanimous opinion of women who knew both husband and wife indicate that the failure to procreate was fortuitous and deplored. Certainly the picture of several little Holmeses tearing through the stately house is an intriguing one.

At any rate, as the years went by, the lives of Wendell and Fanny became more stylized and the pattern became more rigid, in some ways not unlike that of their neighbor on H Street, Henry Adams, whom Wendell at times was wont to ridicule. Adams wanted political office "on a silver platter," said Holmes to Owen Wister, and, as he told James Rowe, "he never would get down in the sawdust as the rest of us did." Rowe saw hyperbole in this statement and added: "I don't know what sawdust he got down into except for the war."

The Holmeses' houses never would have been featured in *Better Homes and Gardens* as models of the decorating art, yet they gradually assumed the peculiarities and preferences of their owners and emerged as eccentric individuals in their own rights.

One was the summer home at Beverly Farms on the North Shore of Massachusetts Bay, some fifteen miles from Boston. Wendell referred to the house which had belonged to Dr. Holmes as a "box" but it took on greater proportions over the years. Fronted by a substantial lawn and surrounded by shrubbery and rocky outcroppings, it lifted its square frame some distance from the sea, which could be seen in the distance through the foliage. This was Wendell's refuge from the heat of non-air-conditioned Washington and he sought it each year as a hart pants for the waterbrooks. The North Shore was indeed a summertime gold coast; the Cabots, Lodges and Higginsons were within hailing distance but the Holmeses' circumstances, while comfortable, were less lordly than those of the great houses of wealthy Bostonians. With sly humor, Wendell laughed at friends in a nearby town who loftily described their location as "Manchester-by-the-Sea." As he saw it, his locale should have been termed "Beverly-by-the-Depot" since the train station was reasonably close by. While at Beverly Farms, Wendell took his daily walks to chat with the guard at the railroad crossing and the postmaster; he experimented with bicycle riding, and, later, he established a base for his beloved automobile rides into the surrounding country and out on Cape Ann. Here he entertained at lunch Felix and Marion Frankfurter from Cambridge, paid visits to John Hays Hammond, the noted mining engineer, pontificated with devotees such as John Knox of Illinois or Harold Laski and bandied words over tea with intellectual feminine confidantes such as Mrs. Albert J. Beveridge.[45]

The design of the wooden, frame house was undistinguished and the decoration unremarkable, but it was comfortable and commodious. Its most remarkable article of adornment was a wood carving made by Fanny, true to the Bowditch maritime tradition. In later years, Fanny tended to keep the bamboo screens down and the shades drawn.

Wendell spent a great deal of time on the second floor, in his study, reading. He supplemented his own library with books from the Athenaeum in Boston and the local library. He liked to depart from his usual diet of serious reading and dip into a mystery or a French novel. Here too, he examined the petitions for writs of certiorari, or requests to review cases, which the clerk sent up from the Court in Washington.

Each year, when Court business had been finished, the Holmes household made its pilgrimage to Beverly Farms and back. With all its trappings and concerns, it came to take on the character of a Middle Eastern *hegira*. To begin with, Wendell was an edgy traveler; every year he grew more nervous about the details of transportation. Even in formal letters to Pollock, his concern was evident in references to ticket purchases and hotel reservations. They traveled by train and in two stages: from Washington to Boston and then from Boston to Beverly Farms. Wendell always insisted on getting to the Union Station far in advance of the 7:30 p.m. departure time of the Federal Express. As Donald Hiss pictured it, "He would sit in that huge waiting room with 'his women' as he called them and his luggage all around him like some tribal chieftain." On one occasion, he even had his secretary go to the station master to have him open the gates early so that all concerned, including the secretary, two maids and a cook, could get established on the train in good season. When the party was settled and Wendell was sitting in his drawing room, he said to his secretary, "Sonny, this is the way to catch a train!"

The secretary said, "Mr. Justice, did you ever miss a train?"

"No," he answered, "but Fanny did once and she never forgot it!"

When they reached Boston the next morning, the group would go to the Hotel Touraine on Tremont Street for breakfast. Then, while the rest went on to the North Shore, Wendell would meet his old clerk and messenger from the Massachusetts court, Jim Doherty, who would escort Holmes to the courthouse. There he would make a few calls and then head on to Beverly Farms by car or train.

On one of these visits Wendell ruefully noted the quick passage of prominence in the public mind—when a policeman allowed parking in a questionable place for the automobile in which he rode because it was "Jim Doherty's car." "There was a time," he complained, "when they would have said, 'it's Judge Holmes's car.'"

The other Holmes house—1720 I Street, N.W. in Washington—was the principal residence of Wendell and Fanny. Bought in the early days of Wendell's service on the Supreme Court, it was located one block west and two blocks north of the White House, just west of Farragut Square. Although it later took on a sort of aura because of its occupants, it was a rather drab three-story and half-basement townhouse with an unrelieved dark brick facade and a few steps leading up to the front door. It had none of the architectural *brio* that Henry H. Richardson[46] had given to the Hay and Adams houses around the corner on Lafayette Square.

The kitchen was in the half basement and the first floor included a parlor, a midparlor, a dining room, and a glassed-in rear porch. The floor of the front parlor was covered by a dark rug. The heaviness of ponderous leather furniture was only partially relieved by light, Boston-tea-party chairs.[47] And the room was accented with a long, rectangular, gold-framed mirror, Tiffany table lamps, and one of Fanny's embroidered landscape pictures. Behind this room was the smaller mid-parlor, more brightly colored and papered. A visitor would note the dark floor and rugs, pots on the mantel, a classic bas-relief on the wall, and small, bound, collections of books in the cases. Further to the rear was the dining room with its massive spread-footed table and large chairs, the great sideboard holding a mass of silver utensils, a dark rug, a portrait of Dorothy Quincy, Wendell's great-grandmother, and, above the sideboard, a painting of William Lloyd Garrison.[48] In the back wall of the dining room, was a door which opened out to a glassed-in porch. The serving maid came and went through a door to the left, shielded by a screen. Out back, there was a small, city-style yard, graced by a beautiful paulownia tree which bloomed luxuriously. Wendell loved this tree and Catherine Hiss, calling for the first time as a young bride, used it as a conversational ploy to divert Wendell's attention from her intense nervousness at meeting such an awesome figure. In the front parlor Fanny held Monday teas as early-century custom mandated[49] and before the First World War they gave many formal dinners in the dining room.

The third floor contained rooms for guests and servants, but the second floor was the "heart" of the house. At the front were the bath and the bedroom (reduced to military simplicity after Fanny's death), with its white iron bedstead under a dramatic oil portrait of Wendell. Two studies filled the rest of the floor. The secretary sat at a desk in the center of the forward study; on three sides floor-to-ceiling bookcases were crammed with books. From this post, the secretary could easily be summoned through the permanently opened double doors to the rear study. Over the mantel of the fireplace of this forward study, swung the manuscript of Dr. Holmes's *The Last Leaf*.[50] The hinged frame permitted both sides of the manuscript to be read. A telephone, looking out of place because of Wendell's antipathy, stood on a small table under a window in an uncomfortable corner.

Wendell really lived in the rear or second study. Since the Supreme Court then had no separate building and the justices no offices[51] (they even had to carry their box lunches to munch in their restricted court room and robing room on the ground floor of the Capitol), he had all his law books and did all his legal work in this room. Here he read and here he was read to, at first by Fanny and later by a succession of secretaries. One secretary called it a "magnificent" room. With its two windows and southern exposure, it was the brightest room in the house. A large desk[52] was set between the windows with its chair by the eastern one. Under the western window rested a standing desk which had belonged to his grandfather, Judge Jackson, and which is now in the office of the dean of the Harvard Law School. Wendell liked to work at this desk, Dean Erwin N. Griswold, of the Law School has explained, because, in Wendell's words, "nothing conduces to brevity of expression like a weakness in the knees."

In the east wall was a fireplace (where casual notes or drafts of decisions were burned) and over the mantel hung the crossed swords his Grandfather Jackson had used in the Indian Wars, together with a dress sword, a pistol in its holster, a military cap and several belts. Framed prints stood on the mantel shelf—one a Meryon etching.[53] Filling every available bit of wall space—from ceiling to floor—were a mass of other books, mostly reports or legal treatises, many with slips of white paper markers showing over their tops. Beside the large desk sat the leather chair in which Wendell did his recreational reading—if reading dutifully approached can be so lightly termed.

These two residences remained in substantially this form until Wendell's death. With the passage of time, the lives of Wendell and Fanny became ordered in a routine corresponding to the terms of the Supreme Court. They came to town for the opening of the Court term in October and left for the Massachusetts North Shore after the Court adjourned in June. At each locale, too, the minutiae of life were ordered with great exactitude by one who was accustomed to issuing orders from the bench. Exact punctuality was important, and if a secretary was called for at eleven he was not admitted to the presence before that hour.

ROUTINE

Wendell rode to the Capitol and back in his carriage until 1925, when, through Fanny's secret machinations, an automobile suddenly appeared at 1720 I Street. He probably would never have purchased one on his own, but after considerable grousing, Wendell accepted it. Eventually the family car became one of his most valued possessions. At the same time, he knew he needed exercise and recreation and his daily walk with his secretary became a prominent item in his routine. He had never been much of a hand at traditional or organized games, but he did feel the need to move his limbs and air his lungs after a day in cigar-smoke in his study. A series of routes were charted in his mind, and as he and his young companion left the house on I Street he would select the course they would stroll.

Barton Leach describes the routes:

> My most regular duty was to take him to walk from five to six, after his return from the Court. We either went "around Cape Horn," which meant to the corner of Connecticut Avenue and 17th Street; or we went to the "infernal regions," which was the negro district in the direction away from the Capitol where

colored children in large quantities played in the street; or we went around by the White House which walk had no name in particular. It was on these walks that he would unburden his mind of whatever was in it—about the cases—about the judges—about his reading—about people, or about life in general.

As he grew older, the regular walks became more difficult for Wendell and by the time Thomas G. Corcoran had joined the household in 1926, Wendell had begun to work in the regular automobile rides which gave him a greater scope of activity and became a great satisfaction of his last years. As with his walks, he developed a series of regular runs which gratified his interest in nature and in the Civil War events in which he had participated.

"About once a week, the justice and I used to take an automobile ride," Corcoran has said, "and sometimes we'd ride over into Virginia. As we went along the Lee Highway, we'd see the signs which we'd stop to examine, saying that here one hundred Confederates stopped two thousand Federal troops or fifty Confederates stopped a regiment of Federal troops, and things like that. He would fume and fuss inwardly and keep quiet as long as he could and then, finally, he'd bust out: 'Well, they knocked the shit out of us, but we won the goddam war, didn't we?' "

He selected a variety of companions for his drives. He always enjoyed the company of pretty young women and one of these fellow tourists, Florence Hollister, vividly remembers these excursions. She was then Florence Wigglesworth, the bride of "Wig" Wigglesworth, the Massachusetts congressman and former Harvard quarterback, who was the son of Fanny's sister, Mary Catherine.

My telephone would ring and his secretary would say, "Could you be ready in half an hour? The justice would like to take a drive." I would say, "Yes." I don't think I ever said "No" because I realized that it was a privilege to have these drives with him and we covered many areas of Washington I'd never known before.

I went several times with him to Fort Stevens out near Military Road where he had seen Lincoln at the battle and where the ramparts can still be seen. Another trip was to go out by the Madeira School in Virginia and as near as we could get to Ball's Bluff to show me where he was wounded. Then, he took me more than once to a small cemetery on Georgia Avenue beyond the Walter Reed Hospital where forty Union soldiers who were killed in the defense of nearby Fort Stevens are buried. It was something that meant a lot to him.

We also visited in the Arlington National Cemetery the mass grave of Civil War unknown soldiers which is near the Custis-Lee Mansion. Two thousand, one hundred and eleven Union soldiers are buried there and the inscription on the memorial stone says that "their remains could not be identified, but their names and deaths are recorded in the archives of their country." He called the inscription "one of the most moving I've ever read," and added, "Can you imagine a greater gift than that? You not only gave your life, but your identity as well."

I also visited the Rock Creek Cemetery with him to look at the St. Gaudens memorial to Clover Adams, the wife of Henry Adams, and popularly called "Grief." This was a favorite stopping place for him. He felt that this was the greatest statue he had ever seen. He would sit on the adjoining seat and study the figure which he loved so much.

I remember one other drive we took which went up the gorge of Rock Creek Park far beyond the Connecticut Avenue viaduct. He wanted to show me the enormous boulders in the Park at that point. . . . It interested me at that time, and still does, to see how catholic his interests were. He was very interested in geology which you wouldn't have thought was one of his things.

During our rides, he would enjoy talking and I was conscious of the fact that I was hearing from someone whose words were very memorable. He was a brilliant conversationalist.

The Fort Stevens referred to by Florence Hollister deserves further attention. It was situated just north of Military Road off Georgia Avenue, then known as the Seventh Street Road and the principal entrance to the District from the north. This is the closest point the Confederates got to the White house, a distance of five miles. In July 1864, as a diversion to relieve the pressure on Richmond, Robert E. Lee had sent General Jubal Early up the Shenandoah Valley, across the Potomac and through Frederick, to chance a raid against Washington. He was delayed for a day by General Lew Wallace at the Monocacy River, but on July tenth, he had twenty thousand men encamped at Rockville, ready to strike. Meantime, however,

LINCOLN AT FORT STEVENS. Plaque on the parapet of Fort Stevens offering imaginative rendering of events on July 12, 1864 when Wendell told the president to get down in no uncertain terms.

Grant, realizing Lee's strategy, gave orders to rush seasoned veterans from Virginia to the Capital for its defense. Among these was Wendell, now a captain in the Sixth Corps under General Horatio C. Wright. By the twelfth, these troops were manning Fort Stevens. General Early was halted and then sent into full retreat.

During the fighting on the eleventh and twelfth, Abraham Lincoln, once with his wife, visited Fort Stevens. Some years ago an incident on the latter day was publicized by Alexander Woolcott, the critic and columnist. As Wendell was going about his duties at the fort, he noticed a tall man wearing a stovepipe hat mount and walk along the parapet. He was a perfect target for the aggressive rebel sharpshooters. Not knowing who the man was, Wendell yelled at him, "Get down, you goddamned fool, or you'll get shot." The man got down below the parapet and nothing untoward happened. A bronze plaque at Fort Stevens memorializes the Lincoln visit and shows an admonitory soldier at the president's arm, but does not identify him.

Wendell revisited the fort at different times with the Hisses, Howe, and Rowe, as well as with Florence Wigglesworth. Although he described to Howe the scene he had seen as he had ridden out from Washington—meeting ramshackle vehicles and hordes of people fleeing south from the enemy—only to Alger Hiss and Rowe did he claim to have been the soldier who shouted the warning to the president. Hiss said that Wendell expressed embarrassment that he had acted as he had to the chief executive.

At any rate, the place became a place of pilgrimage to him in his constant reliving of the events of the Civil War days.

The automobile also afforded Wendell greater scope for indulging his intense love of nature. He always watched for and recorded the first budding of the cherry trees around the Tidal Basin. Said one secretary:

> He was very sensitive to nature and the change of seasons. Each spring he noticed the first violet or crocus and the first robin or blue bird. Driving through Rock Creek Park—it might be in February or March—if he saw a wild flower, he'd have Charlie, the chauffeur, stop the car and he'd get out and scramble up the bank and make an apostrophe to the flower which might be a crocus. If it were, he'd address it as "Little Croaker." These

were very important events to him. He had a keen sense of
nature and beauty.

NOTES ON THE PERSONA

[1] Leslie Scott (1869–1950) and his wife were intimate friends of Wendell
who had been a guest at their house. Scott was Lord Justice of Appeal (1935–
48).

[2] Emma Alice Margaret (Margot) Asquith (1864–1945), second wife of H. H.
Asquith, Prime Minister and First Earl of Oxford.

[3] Lady Frances Horner (1842–1927), wife of Sir John (Francis Fortesque)
Horner.

[4] Howe, *Holmes-Laski Letters*, p. 941 (1927).

[5] Alger Hiss (1904–   ), lawyer, secretary to Wendell in 1929–30, counsel for
various government entities; U.S. executive for organizing Dumbarton Oaks
conference on formation of United Nations and technical advisor to U.S.
delegation to Yalta Conference, 1944; Secretary-General, Organizing Conference of the United Nations, 1945; Defendant in *U.S.* v. *Hiss*, 1949, the noted
perjury case.

[6] W. Barton Leach (1900–1971), secretary to Wendell in 1924–25; member of
Harvard Law School faculty, 1930–69; noted entertainer and singer of witty
songs, many composed by himself, which he accompanied on the accordion.

[7] Charles Sydney Hopkinson (1869–1962), Harvard '91, studied in Boston
and Paris, became a noted portrait painter, doing studies of Harvard Presidents
Eliot, Lowell and Conant. Recipient of innumerable medals and awards.

[8] John Lockwood was secretary to Wendell in 1928–29 and was later a New
York lawyer, counsel and advisor to Governor Nelson Rockefeller and lawyer
for various Rockefeller interests.

[9] Augustin Derby was secretary to Wendell in 1906–07 and later became
professor of law at the New York University School of Law and dean of the law
school of the University of Virginia. His "Recollections of Mr. Justice Holmes"
appeared in *New York University Law Quarterly Review* 12:345 (1935). The
quotation from this article is reprinted with permission of the *Review*.

[10] Gutzon Borglum (1871–1941), American sculptor who planned and
started the Mount Rushmore Memorial in South Dakota. He also sculpted the
head of Lincoln in the Rotunda of the Capitol in Washington.

[11] Florence Hollister, widow of Fanny Holmes's nephew, Richard Bowditch
Wigglesworth, who was a member of Congress and ambassador to Canada.

[12] Katharine L. Bundy, widow of Harvey L. Bundy, a Holmes secretary in
1914–15, mother of McGeorge Bundy, one-time presidential assistant to President Kennedy and William P. Bundy, assistant secretary of state under President Johnson.

[13] In the Civil War, there were great losses, Wendell told Einstein, "when
troops stood within a few paces letting into one another." Peabody, *The
Holmes-Einstein Letters*, vol. 2, p. 101.

[14] Peabody, *The Holmes-Einstein Letters*, vol. 3, p. 272.

Lewis Einstein (1877–1949), American diplomat, author, party of the second
part in extended correspondence with Wendell cited above, father of Lady
Tweeddale, also a correspondent of Wendell.

[15] James Barr Ames, dean of the Harvard Law School had been a varsity
baseball player and one wonders if the discrepancy in physical co-ordination

between him and Wendell contributed to the coolness which existed in the relations between these two sons of Harvard. Howe, *The Proving Years*, p. 231.

[16] Austin W. Scott, fabled, brilliant and beloved professor of law at Harvard Law School (1909–61), outstanding authority on trusts.

[17] Sayre Macneil, professor of law, Harvard Law School (1926–33).

[18] Sir Frederick Pollock (1845–1937), distinguished British legal scholar, author of *Principles of Contract* and numerous legal studies, intimate friend of Wendell through their fascinating correspondence over fifty-eight years, contained in Mark DeWolfe Howe, ed., *Holmes-Pollock Letters* (Cambridge: Harvard University Press, 1941).

[19] Resourceful and supportive Irish-born head of Wendell's household after the death of Fanny.

[20] Mark DeWolfe Howe (1906–1967), distinguished Boston man of letters, professor of law at Harvard Law School (1946–67), scrupulous editor of *Holmes-Pollock Letters* and *Holmes-Laski Letters* and author of the definitive *Justice Holmes: The Shaping Years* and *The Proving Years*. Howe tragically died in 1967 before this biography was completed.

[21] Alpha Delta Phi, a national fraternity of which Wendell was a member, now a local club at Harvard, known as the Fly Club. Porcellian is a "final" club at Harvard. Wendell was a member. It it still extant with a clubhouse at Harvard Square.

[22] Owen Wister, *Roosevelt: The History of a Friendship* (New York: Macmillan, 1930), p. 129.

[23] Jean-Adrien-Antoine-Jules Jusserand (1855–1932), man of letters, author of *Literary History of the English People* (in French), French ambassador to Washington from 1902–25).

[24] Leonard Wood (1860–1927), a Harvard-trained doctor of medicine was military governor of Cuba (1899–1902); commander of the Rough Riders in the Spanish War, commander of the U.S. forces in the Philippines (1906–09); chief of staff (1910–14). Pushed unsuccessfully for the Republican presidential nomination in 1920.

[25] Henry Cabot Lodge (1850–1924), Harvard 1871, historian, member of House of Representatives (1886–1893); member of Senate (1893–1924); chairman of Senate Committee on Foreign Relations whence he led a successful fight against ratification of League of Nations Treaty (1920), intimate friend and advisor to Theodore Roosevelt.

[26] Ellen Maury Slayden (1860–1926) was the wife of Texas Congressman James Luther Slayden who served the San Antonio District for twenty-two years. Her sharp and vivid journal, *Washington Wife* (New York: Harper & Row, 1962) has been called "one of the best contemporary records of the period between" 1897 and 1919. She was the aunt of Rep. Maury Maverick.

[27] The solicitor general was John W. Davis who filled that position from 1913–18.

[28] Here Wendell paralleled Dr. Samuel Johnson who asked Mrs. Mary Knowles: "Have we heard all that a disciple of Confucius, all that a Mahometan, can say for himself?" W. Jackson Bate, *Samuel Johnson* (New York: Harcourt Brace Jovanovich, 1975), pp. 90–91.

[29] Ellen Maury Slayden, *Washington Wife—Journal of Ellen Maury Slayden* (New York: Harper & Row, 1962), entry of February 11, 1917, p. 272.

[30] John Knox, "A Luncheon With Justice Oliver Wendell Holmes and Alger Hiss," *The Brief, Phi Delta Phi Quarterly* (Washington, D.C.), 1976.

Knox is a devoted Holmes scholar. Ph.B. University of Chicago 1930; J.D. Northwestern 1934; LL.M. Harvard 1936.

[31] Howe, *The Proving Years,* p. 273.

[32] Jimmy Lake and Helen Giblo, *Footlights, Fistfights and Femmes* (New York: Vantage Press, 1957), p. 188.

[33] Wister, *Roosevelt,* p. 134.

[34] Sholem Asch, *Three Cities*—a trilogy about Jews in World War I. Originally published in 1933.

[35] Diary of Mark DeWolfe Howe. Harvard Law School Library, quoted with permission of the librarian and Mrs. Molly (Howe) Adams.

[36] W. Barton Leach, "Recollections of a Holmes Secretary," unpublished transcript of a talk prepared for delivery at a meeting of Holmes secretaries. Harvard Law School Library.

[37] Mark DeWolfe Howe, unpublished diary, February 21, 1934, p. 25.

[38] Interview with Mrs. John Coakley (Annie Mary Donnellan), describing the household in the late twenties.

[39] James H. Rowe, Jr. (1909–1984), Montana native, graduate of Harvard College and Law School, secretary to Wendell in 1934 and 1935 and thus the last of the thirty secretaries, attorney in governmental agencies, special assistant to President Franklin Roosevelt, naval officer, close advisor to President Johnson, Washington insider and law partner of Thomas G. Corcoran.

[40] From 1902 to 1913, Wendell's salary was $10,000 a year, without income tax. The minimum and maximum income tax rates were: 1 percent to 7 percent in 1913–15; 6 percent to 7 percent (over a million) in 1918; 1⅛ percent (after earned income credit) to 25 percent (over a million) in 1927.

[41] Wendell bequeathed his residual estate of over $250,000 to the United States of America. This was the largest such bequest to the time of his death in 1935. The sorry history of the fund created by this bequest constitutes a disservice to Wendell's memory and a powerful argument against emulating his generous gesture.

[42] *Historical Statistics of the United States,* U.S. Department of Commerce, Bureau of the Census, 1975, p. 1095.

To provide material for comparable values see: "The Consumer Price Index for All Urban Consumers, 1800–1984," *Historical Statistics,* U.S. Department of Commerce, Bureau of the Census, 1985.

[43] *Compañia de Tabácos de Filipinas* v. *Collector* (1904), 275 U.S. 87: 100.

[44] Howe, *The Proving Years,* p. 8, note 17.

[45] Widow of Albert J. Beveridge, U.S. Senator from Indiana from 1899 to 1911, leader in the Progressive Party and winner of the Pulitzer Prize for his *The Life of John Marshall.* She was one of Wendell's most intimate friends.

[46] Henry Hobson Richardson (1838–1886) was an American architect who achieved international fame. He earned his first great notice in Boston by winning a design competition for Trinity Church in 1872.

[47] Boston-tea-party chairs were so described in a description of the furnishings of the house which accompany a series of eleven photographs of the interior of 1720 I Street taken in 1935 shortly after Wendell's death.

[48] William Lloyd Garrison (1805–1879), journalist, reformer and antislavery activist, organizer of the first society for the immediate abolition of slavery. His life was endangered by a mob in Boston in 1835.

[49] Certain days of the week were set aside by custom when members of the Cabinet, Supreme Court, and Congress wives were "at home" for callers. The day for the Supreme Court wives was Monday.

[50] Holmes, *Poetical Works of Oliver Wendell Holmes,* p. 1.

[51] The present Supreme Court building designed by Cass Gilbert was completed in 1935. Prior to that time, the Court sat on the ground floor and later the

second (principal) floor of the Capitol.

[52] Wendell told Barton Leach that he never used the large desk which had been his father's because he "didn't like the old man."

[53] Charles Meryon (1821–1868), French etcher who produced distinctive and sharply drawn views of Paris, often peopled by fantastic creatures. He was mentally unstable and destroyed some of his most beautiful creations in an *accés de folie*.

Fanny

Of all the considerable assets with which Wendell was blessed, none was more valuable than his wife, Fanny Bowditch Dixwell Holmes. "She was a remarkable woman," said Tommy Corcoran, "in some ways more remarkable than he, and, because of her, his life was very different from what it would have been without her. In many respects, she was stronger than he and she guided him through his times of crisis with the courage that accepts and faces the problems of life." Aware of his nervous temperament and inherited moodiness, she very subtly maintained the balance in his life that was necessary for his happiness.

Fanny and Wendell knew each other from their earliest days. Born in Cambridge, she was three months older than he and the eldest of six children born to Mary Ingersoll and Epes (Dicky) Dixwell, the former head of the Boston Latin School. Later, Dixwell became director of his own private Latin school which Wendell attended and was reputed to be the best in Boston. On her father's side, Fanny was descended from John Dixwell, one of the signers of the execution decree of Charles I. Her maternal grandfather was Nathaniel Bowditch, of Salem, author of the world-famous and still-used *Practical Navigator,* an intrepid pilot who, by dead reckoning, one Christmas Eve safely brought his ship past the dangerous Baker's Island rocks and into Salem Harbor.

Throughout Fanny's childhood, the large Dixwell house at 58 Garden Street, Cambridge, hummed with activity. Epes, himself, played the flute and sang Scotch songs at weekly musical gatherings. He regularly acted as host to a group of intellectuals from the neighboring Harvard community who called themselves the Scientific Club and gathered at stated intervals to discuss the burning questions of the day.

When Wendell marched away with the Twentieth Regiment, Massachusetts Volunteers in September 1861, Fanny was among the damsels who bade farewell with fluttered handkerchiefs. She faithfully corresponded with him during his three years of service. When he was wounded and came back to Beacon Street to convalesce, she came to visit, and on one occasion read him aloud the poem General Frederick W. Lander[1] had written about the bravery of the officers of the Twentieth Regiment.[2] As a gallant, wounded officer, Wendell was the toast of Boston and there were many ladies beside Fanny who brought presents and offered tribute to the preening captain. In his autobiography, Francis Biddle[3] cited the remark of his wife's aunt: As a Boston girl, she was "brought up under the romance of Wendell Holmes going to war and his return."

After the war, as he studied law, was admitted to the Massachusetts Bar, engaged in active practice, and wrote and edited on legal subjects, Wendell kept in touch with Fanny. At the same time, there were other young ladies to court the *beau idéal* and he was hardly an ardent swain in pressing his suit. Biddle cites William James[4] who knew Fanny ("Decidedly A-1 and the best girl I have known") and alleged that "that villain Wendell Holmes has been keeping her all to himself out in Cambridge for the last eight years." But, at length, as Corcoran put it, "She was the one who got him." Pressed by his Uncle John, he made his proposal which she accepted. At age thirty-one, they were married in Christ Church, Cambridge by Phillips Brooks[5] on June 17, 1872.

After the ceremony, with legal pedantry Wendell told Fanny that he had affirmed "with all my wordly goods, I thee endow." But he added that *endow* as a word of art refers only to real estate—of which he had none. Not only did he not have real estate; he had few worldly goods of any kind. They took no wedding trip and moved in with the elder Holmeses on the third floor at 296 Beacon Street.

From that day forward, Fanny subordinated her life to Wendell's and sought only his happiness and success. Whether living with her in-laws or, later, in the rooms they took above the drugstore at 10 Beacon Street, next to the Athenaeum, she self-sacrificingly preserved his equilibrium and maintained the atmosphere in which he could work.

With his powerful ambition and desire to fashion an identity apart from that of his father, Wendell had dedicated his life single-mindedly to creating a work which would bring him fame before he was forty. Soon he was to begin working, in addition to his normal legal work, on the completion of *The Common Law,* a master work which would guarantee the fame which he purposefully sought.

The sacrifice of a wedding trip symbolized the scholarly dedication of their life together as did her wedding present to him of a first edition of the *Leviathan* of Thomas Hobbes,[6] the materialistic English philosopher. Three weeks after the wedding, he was reading Kant's *Eléments Métaphysiques de la Doctrine du Droit.*[7] Eventually, when the results of his reading began to take shape in his great treatise, she pitched in to read proofs and to discuss with him the problems he faced as he turned out his copy.

Fanny acted as both an energy source and a balance wheel for her more mercurial husband. Although Wendell had been a fighting infantry officer through three years of bloody battles, it was she who stiffened his backbone to make the great decisions in his life. When Governor John Davis Long,[8] nearing the end of his term, had allotted Wendell a few hours to decide whether or not to leave the Harvard Law School faculty and accept nomination to the Massachusetts Supreme Judicial Court, it was Fanny who went dashing around Boston in a carriage with Wendell's partner, George Shattuck, to tie up loose ends. Twenty years later when he was vacillating about leaving the position of state chief justice to become a "side judge" in Washington, she firmly asserted that he must accept Theodore Roosevelt's nomination; she immediately assumed the burden of making physical arrangements for a radical change of venue.

Fanny shared and understood Wendell's interests in fields outside the law; in these areas her gifts complemented his life. She had a very delicate artistic sensibility and tremendous manual skill. Her embroidered colored pictures were widely known; her touch was so light and skillful that her landscapes and seascapes compared with oil paintings in their scope and impact.[9]

A *Boston Advertiser* critic, reviewing her exhibit of embroidered panels at the Boston Art Museum in 1880, called them "probably the most remarkable needlework ever done." A reviewer in *The Nation,* writing of a New York showing of her work, called her "an American artist of noticeable qualities," and a writer in *The American Architect and Building News* described her work as "a difficult enterprise, of course, and one not to be lightly undertaken by a person possessed of less exquisite taste, and less accomplished drawing, and a less pleasing sense of color than are possessed by Mrs. Holmes."[10] The judicious and sophisticated Oscar Wilde, after an evening at 10 Beacon Street, described Fanny—a trifle inaccurately, since she was not a weaver—as "that Penelope of New England" and mentioned her "silken pictures I found so beautiful."

Characteristically and regrettably, in her last years Fanny had her pictures destroyed, asserting that she did not relish the idea that nieces "must cherish the works of departed aunts."

Fanny also had the capacity to follow Wendell in his dedicated and even obsessive exploration of all types of literature. This identification was intensified when, during his service on the Massachusetts court and upon the advice of a physician, Wendell gave up reading at night to save his eyesight. Fanny then began the practice—which ended only with her final illness—of reading aloud to him after dinner while he played a form of solitaire called "Canfield." In this additional way, she contributed to his happiness and strengthened the bonds that joined them.

Beside her manual and artistic skills and her appreciation of great literature, Fanny had the ability, both orally and in writing, to use language with a vigor and sharpness that would now qualify her to be a columnist or script writer. Unfortunately, examples of her literary competence are sparse, but titillating samples appear in the diary she kept of their trip to Europe in the summer of 1874.[11] Her descriptions of traveling Americans, Anglican bishops, British *grandes dames,* and prominent politicians have a bite which fully supports her characterization by Mark Howe as a diarist with a "corrosive eye."

Of one American couple she wrote: "I have seldom seen a man who combined in such small quarters such a gigantic defect of manners, mind and heart linked to so fitting a partner as a wife." She described a noble host as "a twinkling hippopotamus." She reported another scene as follows:

The Dean very disagreeable in black stockings, long coat, black sash and ribbon round his neck. Overheard some joke between him and two or three fat old ladies covered with feathers, lace and chains about "St. Peter's daughter—and he, you know, was not a married man"—at which point up went the fans and the Dean's hand to conceal his face from his own joke—altogether the whole impression not of a gospel of humility and simplicity. Fat old ladies with immense bosoms and larger stomachs both adorned with gold and precious stones. One thin old lady with a cap and veil of heavy black lace with a red feather held in place by a diamond cluster, a black satin overdress and red satin petticoat and a roll of white cardboard tied up with red ribbon and attached to her belt by a red ribbon which roll she used for an ear trumpet.

Clearly, a great journalist was lost when Fanny failed to continue her practice of this demanding art.

Fanny also had an amazing sensitivity to external influences of a physical nature. Wendell told one secretary of Fanny's ability to return home after an afternoon's absence, move about the drawing room, and say "So-and-so was here." She could make the identification from the aroma of a cigar or the odor of a perfume.

Fanny could never be categorized simply as a devoted and self-effacing helpmeet. She was more than that; in fact at times such as when they moved to Washington, she was the effective party. Of course, she felt trepidation, as Wendell did, about the departure from staid Boston to the national scene, but she could envisage the opportunities that would open up for Wendell and she was willing to make the leap. In addition, a feeling of reserve between her and her family made the separation less difficult. A severe illness—rheumatic fever—in 1896 had changed her appearance and lessened her energy, but she felt "cabin'd, cribb'd and confined"[12] in the city where the parental shadow of Dr. Holmes, poet and wit, diminutive as it was, had always tended to keep Wendell in its shade.

The correctness of Fanny's judgment about accepting the Supreme Court appointment was amply proven after they moved to Washington in 1902; she, as well as he, expanded and blossomed in the more ample and relaxed atmosphere of the Capital. If not beautiful or stylish, she was brilliant and witty and she became a striking figure in society during T.R.'s reign. For a time, Wendell and Fanny were intimates of the president and dined in the White House with regularity as part of a group, largely Harvard, called "the Roosevelt Familiars" by Owen Wister. Included were the Henry Cabot Lodges, the Winthrop Chanlers, and the Grant La Farges,[13] and the close relations continued until Wendell voted against the administration position in the *Northern Securities Company* antitrust case. At this point, the simplistic president roared that he could carve a judge with more backbone out of a banana and vowed that Wendell and Fanny would never again "darken the door" of the White House. Here Fanny was the moderating influence. She joshed the president out of his obduracy, but relations were never again the same.

Wister, referring to the "ladies who came to the Roosevelt *salon,*" included "Mrs. Wendell Holmes, her quaint and wholly individual raciness, her beautiful embroidery like none other" and classed her with the others in this élite group as "an accomplished woman of the world, her native wits seasoned by experience with many people and familiarity with many books, and well able to hold up her end in the talk."[14]

In this period of the ascendancy of the "Dude Cowboy," Wendell and Fanny "entertained widely" and were similarly entertained themselves. Not only did Fanny supervise a host of formal dinners at I Street, but she presided over the mandatory "at homes" prescribed for wives of the Supreme Court justices and of other government officials. Her wit became famous and it was to T.R. that she delivered the most noted *mot* of all. Fanny had told him that she had met a number of official wives since her arrival in the city. Roosevelt asked her if she found them interesting. "Mr. President," said Fanny, "Washington is full of famous men and the women they married when they were young."

According to Richard W. Hale,[15] a close family friend, it was at this period that she "vamped" William Jennings Bryan,[16] and Hale concluded that her opinion of the prominent Democrat was "definitely favorable" in contrast to that of her husband. There is provocative ambiguity in the use of the jazz-age verb.

Fanny could be forceful and courageous as well as acerbic. She proved this some years later during the sovereignty of the "Professor from Princeton."[17] As one secretary told the story, the incident happened at a White House dinner the Wilsons gave for the justices of the Supreme Court. During the dinner

> a waiter spilled soup on the snowy shirtfront of Mr. Justice Day,[18] a man noted for his modesty. Of course, the waiter was horrified and the justice was quietly trying to clean himself up with his napkin. Wilson began to upbraid the waiter and this just confused and embarrassed Day all the more and drew greater attention to the accident. Finally, Mrs. Holmes turned to Wilson and said, "Mr. President, you know there are some things one just doesn't talk about. Meaning: "Shut up! Leave the poor man alone!" Of course, Wilson subsided. Holmes told me about that incident. He was so proud of her.

Wendell was not an admirer of Wilson and in October 1914 described to Lewis Einstein the president's "drooling business of suggesting prayers for peace" and speculated that this proposal "meant votes from Methodists and Baptists."

Fanny showed her mettle in another exchange described to Francis Biddle by none other than Franklin Roosevelt who was in Washington as an assistant secretary of the Navy in the Wilson administration: "Ambassador Bakhmeteff, who was notorious for repeating salacious stories to ladies . . . tried one on Mrs. Holmes . . . and she went him one better without the slightest mark of surprise or disapproval. He did not afterward tell dirty stories to American women."[19]

World War I was a watershed period for Fanny. She still felt the effects of the rheumatic fever of 1896 and in 1919 she had another illness which left her "easily pulled down," as Wendell described it. Her appearance had become less attractive. Mrs. James B. Ayer[20] told Mark Howe that "she really did look like a monkey with a long upper lip, darting black eyes and the restless manner of a small bird." Her very early photos show her to have been a round-cheeked, pretty girl, but it is impossible to document the change in her features over the years since she was eventually adamant in her refusal to be photographed. In the Holmes collection at the Harvard Law School, there is only one picture of Fanny in the years of their marriage and that is an enlarged snapshot of a picture taken at Beverly Farms by Mrs. John G. Palfrey,[21] showing Fanny in a side view with gray hair. It is so dark that the viewer can hardly discern her features. For a long time, she fended off people who tried to get her to have a picture taken and then, finally, according to Katharine Bundy, she said, "All right, I'll give you my picture." She passed around as of her a picture of an old Buddha photographed somewhere in the Far East.

After her illnesses, Fanny developed a sensitivity to light and kept certain areas of their houses dark. Isabella Wigglesworth, the wife of Fanny's nephew, has described the house at Beverly Farms: "Oh that house! I wish you could have seen it then. Not one ray of light penetrated it. Everything was hermetically sealed. There was a porch with rattan curtains that were rolled down to the floor and shades drawn in the windows of the house and electric lights going all the time."

As her looks deteriorated, her dress and toilette became more bizarre. "She had deep sunken eyes," said Isabella Wigglesworth of Fanny in her later years, "and she never made any attempt to do anything with herself. She had her hair skinned back. She was just the way she was. No change. In her youth, she was just beautiful, but I guess she just decided she couldn't compete with Wendell's beautiful young lady friends and that she was just going to be herself—which she was—and she won out." It took Fanny to voice an adequate description of herself. As early as the first days in Washington, she told a friend that she looked "like an abandoned farm in Maine."

Fanny had a highly developed sense of humor which stood her in good stead in coping with the vagaries of their married life. She loved practical jokes, especially if they made Wendell look ridiculous. She would set out unlightable matches for him to struggle with as he tried to light his cigar. On April Fools' Day, she put an overturned ink bottle and king-sized artificial blot on the white page to horrify him when he came to pick up the fresh draft of his latest opinion. She set the fake cockroach in the flour barrel so Wendell would bespatter himself as he tried to remove it.

An example of Fanny's light touch—and her interest in children—is this letter written to the children of John Palfrey one Christmas: "We have a suspicion that fairies live in the walls of this house and we are going to try to catch one and send him to your house—to tell you that we wish you all a very Happy New Year."

She possessed what Alger Hiss called "a very teasing, charming, light-hearted gayety and he [Wendell] enjoyed the jokes that she would play on him. He told me these stories and he would repeat them to the other secretaries. He said that one reason he had a new secretary every year was so that he could retell these stories." She had a particular skill—and took a particular pleasure—in bringing him abruptly to earth when, through stuffiness or vanity, he had got up on his high horse.

In many ways, the relationship between Wendell and Fanny had a naive quality about it. Charlie Buckley, their coachman and later chauffeur, told one secretary that when he took them for drives they would kick one another under the lap robe like flirting adolescents.

"They were like children," was Mary Donnellan's appraisal of their relationship. "Very nice."

Several people have recounted the story of the lost book. One morning before he went to court, Wendell was checking something and wanted a book which he couldn't find in its proper place on the shelves. He rushed off to court saying, "Send a telegram to every secretary saying, 'You thief, return such-and-such a volume. It's not in its place.'" When he got back from the court, he found a piece of paper pinned to the spine of the book—which was two places down the shelf. A note on the paper written by Fanny said: "I'm a very old man and I have many troubles, most of which never occur."

Wendell liked to give his imagination free rein and to indulge in persiflage whenever the opportunity afforded itself. Fanny just as eagerly seized the chance to deflate the balloon of pomposity. Richard Hale has described one such occasion:

It was my wife's first appearance in Beverly after our marriage. I feel temperate when I say of the Justice that he was always willing to make a favorable impression upon a new bird of the opposite sex. He fixed her attention. Then a steady stream of the deepest philosophy poured from his lips. The beautiful sonorous voice flowed on. The listener tried to conceal her panic and the agony with which she was striving to have an intelligent comment ready at the peroration. But concealment from "the Mrs." was impossible. Just at the critical zenith of words her phrase shot out like a needle against a balloon:
"George!—You do talk pretty!"[22]

Biddle writes of another similar incident. Wendell, Fanny, and the secretary had taken tea at I Street after the men had finished a walk on the canal tow path. With an appreciative listener, Wendell was discussing philosophers and dissecting their theories while expatiating on his own. He had been declaiming for some time when he said, "For, after all, the business of philosophy is to show that we are not fools for doing what we want to do. The judge looked at the secretary, who smiled. Mrs. Holmes bit off a thread. She had been sewing. 'Pass me the scissors, Wendell,' she said."[23]

Fanny enjoyed anything which broke the routine. She loved to go to fires and, in their Boston days, spectators could often see this middle-aged pair hurrying after the clanging fire apparatus on its way to the scene. Isabella Wigglesworth once told of an incident that illustrated this capacity for spontaneous enjoyment. Wendell and Fanny had taken her young husband and herself out to dinner at the Willard Hotel. When they got back to I Street, they were greeted by the secretary who said, "Mrs. Holmes, there's a bat in the bathroom." "Oh, what fun," Fanny shouted. Whereupon she grabbed an umbrella, leaped upstairs, and banged on the walls and the plumbing fixtures. "I don't think there was a bat at all," Wigglesworth commented. "She just put on a terribly good act. We all had such a laugh."

Although she withdrew more and more into her privacy, Fanny never lost her interest in people and, as one observer said, "She loved gossip." She possessed a fund of affection which she lavished upon the young women and men in contact with the household. She had the capacity to open up and be intimate in a way her more formal husband could not—even though he experienced intense emotional surges at times. As the young Washington wife of a Holmes secretary, Katharine Bundy got to know Fanny quite well. "She was a lovable person, really a lovable creature, and very approachable. I loved her." Since Wendell had a rule that secretaries should not be married, the Bundys had held off from taking the final step. But "Mrs. Holmes was very eager to have us married, so she was pushing and pushing." When the young couple told Wendell about their engagement "he was darling about it," and they were married in June in the middle of Harvey Bundy's term of service. Before Katharine Bundy came down to Washington, Harvey wrote her several revealing letters about Wendell and

Fanny. He described Fanny as "Mrs. Holmes who has spent her life in devotion to him. Without her he never could have been so great. The sacrifice in such a life work as that of Mrs. Holmes may not be noble for such a woman, but it is no mean career."

He later described a session with Fanny: "I had the best time this afternoon talking with Mrs. Holmes. We gossiped for an hour or more. She said she told the Justice if my work wasn't done at any time, it would be because she bothered me. She really seems to like to come in and talk to me and I know I love it. She doesn't wear her heart on her sleeves. She's the most lovable woman and sensitive and high strung. New England all the way through and always thinking of something to do for other people."

One of the results of Fanny's career of self-abnegation was the development of an excessive interest in the lives of those people with whom she did have contact. In Isabella Wigglesworth's view: "She was extremely curious. She had no life of her own, so she always wanted to know what *I* was doing. I remember a man coming to discuss some matter with me and I said, 'We can't talk in the house because she's just like a kid, trying to hear every word we say, and I don't want her to.' So, we went up to a bench in the bushes above the house and sat and talked there."

An insight into Fanny's affection for people and the nature of her relationship with Wendell can be found in Joseph P. Lash's *From the Diaries of Felix Frankfurter*. The playwright Garson Kanin describes Frankfurter's report of the Holmeses' reaction to Frankfurter's engagement announcement:

Holmes jumped up and shouted for Fanny. "Dickie!" he called, "Dickie bird!" (F. F. gets up at this point to give a brilliant imitation of Mrs. Holmes coming into the room. She was old and infirm and moved without lifting her feet from the floor.) As she came in, Holmes said to F. F., "Tell her! Tell her!"

"I'm going to marry Miss Denman," said F. F.

Fanny said nothing, but turned and slipped out of the room. He and Holmes thought this behavior odd. Somewhat embarrassed they went on talking about other things. All at once, Fanny returned. She held out her fist and asked F. F., "Which do you think she would like? This?" She opened one fist, revealing a piece of jade. "Or this?" She opened another fist which contained a piece of amber. F. F. pointed to the amber and said, "This I think." Fanny handed it to him, turned, shuffled out of the room, and was seen no more that day.

Fanny was particularly interested in the series of young secretaries who came from the Harvard Law School to serve Wendell for a year's stint. She was sensitive to their needs and sought to make them feel at home. Tommy Corcoran has described his first meeting with Fanny at I Street. "Well, Mr. Corcoran," she said, "we know all about you, but what do you know about us?"

Corcoran answered that he had read all about the justice, knew his opinions and was familiar with his engagements in the Civil War.

"That's really unimportant," she said. "I wonder if you know what a Unitarian is."

He said, "Mrs. Holmes, I was in Boston long enough to know what a Unitarian is. It's a reformed kind of Congregationalist."

"You can put it in that complicated way if you want to," she said, "but if you really want to know the simplicity of the thing, it's this: in Boston, you had to be *something* and Unitarian was the least you could be."

Thus was the young Irish-American, Roman Catholic made to feel at home in "that Brahmin house." Corcoran soon became aware that Fanny possessed firmness and judgment along with sensitivity and affection, and that she understood that life was a "risky business." She had even painted in illuminated manuscript style an epitaph written by the Syracusan poet, Theodoridas,[24] from the *Greek Anthology* which demonstrated her understanding of life's chances:

> A shipwrecked sailor buried on this coast
> Bids thee take sail.
> Full many a gallant ship, when we were lost,
> Weathered the gale.

Corcoran discovered that she could be a strong partisan and was not averse to showing it. He cited the story of the first dinner party she gave in Washington. As Yankees, she and Wendell "came into a community which, at that time, was almost completely a Southern, even Confederate, city." In some ways, it had not changed from the war time when Wendell, even though an officer, could not get accommodations at Willard's Hotel because he was a Northerner.

> The Washington society of the day did not favor Union supporters, even though the War Between the States was forty years in the past. Certainly, a brevet colonel, thrice wounded and with three years of hard military combat against the South, was looked upon with social suspicion. Mrs. Holmes, well aware of this when she seated her carefully chosen Southern guests, called their attention to the family portraits on the walls of her dining room. She particularly pointed out William Lloyd Garrison, the famous abolitionist, anathema to the South. The other portraits were in the same vein. She smiled softly at the frozen looks of her guests.

Corcoran found, too, that Fanny had her own standards of social propriety which did not always correspond with those of her husband. In spite of Wendell's close relationship with Brandeis, Fanny had reservations about their fellow Bostonian. When Brandeis, a Jew from Louisville, had graduated from the Harvard Law School as the most brilliant student in its history and had started practice in Boston, Colonel Henry Lee Higginson, head of the United Shoe Corporation and a pillar of society, had gone out of his way to introduce the newcomer in the clubs and in all the proper places to show his support. Alice Brandeis was invited to teas by proper Bostonian ladies, and the couple were fully accepted in that structured society. Higginson gave the Brandeis firm some of his corporate legal business, but when labor organized at the plant and the union called the workers out on strike, Brandeis took the part of the strikers. Fanny did not approve of Brandeis's action, Corcoran asserted. "One just doesn't do this sort of thing," she said. Many other Bostonians shared her views and the violence of their sentiments exploded in passionate opposition to confirmation when Wilson nominated Brandeis to the Supreme Court in 1916.

With increasing physical disabilities, Fanny indulged her natural shyness and reserve and abandoned large-scale social activities. Dedicated as she was to Wendell's happiness, one of the last of her triumphs was the brilliant celebration of his eightieth birthday. She secretly assembled all his former secretaries, grouped them behind the closed doors of the dining room and presented them to his startled eyes when he came downstairs, dressed, as he thought, to go out to dinner. At one time, Wendell had said of her, "She is a very solitary bird, and if her notion of duty did not compel her to do otherwise, she would be an absolute recluse, I think. . . . She and I are a queer contrast in that way, as in many others." Her last years intensified this tendency and justified his analysis. But her withdrawal did not lessen her interest in the household and its comforts. It was she who had the house wired for electricity, who ordered a telephone connected, and had an elevator installed. Wendell acknowledged to Pollock: "If it weren't for my wife, I doubt if I should have any modern improvements." As has been noted, she substituted an automobile for the horse-drawn coupe, a change that Wendell had resisted.

In these declining years, Fanny's thoughts were constantly on Wendell's welfare and, with characteristic realism and forethought, she conceived and carried out a project that immeasurably eased his last years. Realizing that she might well predecease him, she hired and trained a young Irish woman to take her place as best anyone could, and to watch over him if she were gone. Fanny could see that this young woman was sensitive, intelligent, resourceful, and attractive, with a fresh charm she had brought from her native County Roscommon. Her name was Annie Mary Donnellan, known as "Mary." Mary had had some nursing training and began service at I Street as a maid. Her initial attempt at service was not successful; at breakfast she spilled a dish of scrambled eggs in Wendell's lap. With habitual courtliness, he rose to the occasion, went upstairs, put on another coat and trousers, and returned for a second plate of eggs. To Mary's domestic experience, Fanny added a course in Wendell's crotchets, his professional requirements, his dietary preferences, his recreational predilections, and his physical needs. With this instruction, Mary was able to take over Wendell's care and the supervision of the household after Fanny's death—a task Mary performed with great distinction. Through this able surrogate, Fanny planned that her love and devotion would be bestowed upon Wendell as long as he lived.

After Wendell's death, Mary married John Coakley, a contractor, and they became the parents of five children. The characteristic of Fanny that many remembered best was her kindness. "Oh, she was so kind. She used to see that I got off to Mass at Saint Matthew's Cathedral, even though she didn't go to church herself. And when I got back to the house from Mass, she would have ready for me coffee and rolls which she had prepared herself. She was a lovely, thoughtful person."

Early in 1929 in the bathroom of the I Street house, Fanny fell and broke her hip. At her age, the result was inevitable. She died on April thirtieth, aged eighty-eight. To Pollock, Bundy, and others, Wendell repeated, "I am reconciled by the certainty that a continuance of life would have meant only a continuance of pain and suffering of which my wife had too much before the final accident." To Pollock he added, "We have had our share. For sixty years she made life poetry for me and at eighty-eight one must be ready for the end."

Fanny was not "ceremonial," as Isabella Wigglesworth had said, and Wendell had hoped to avoid obsequies. But because Chief Justice Taft and Charles Evans Hughes convinced him that this would be inappropriate, a service was held on May third at the Holmes residence. Wendell read a favorite poem of theirs by Joseph Blanco White, called "To Night." Fanny was buried in Arlington National Cemetery in a plot secured by Taft and next to the site where her husband, Brevet Colonel Holmes, would be laid to rest in another six years.

After her death, the depth of Wendell's feeling for Fanny was evidenced by his frequent automobile tours to Arlington National Cemetery to visit her grave. There, according to Chapman Rose, a secretary, Wendell would get out of the car and walk up to their plot where "in a characteristic gesture, he would rub his hand slowly over the stone of the monument." And on frequent occasions, he would lay a single red rose on her grave.

One may well ask why this remarkable woman has not been of more interest to those who have commented on Wendell's life and works. But Fanny never sought recognition. Her intense shyness and reserve kept her out of the limelight. Her devotion to Wendell fed her dedication to secure for him the fame which he sought and to which she believed him entitled. Finally, there was a not unimportant factor: Wendell was willing, even eager, to accept any applause and bask in any *kudos* which were directed toward the Holmes family.

Emily Brontë left behind her only three not very personal letters and a few French *devoirs;* she never kept a diary and destroyed the manuscripts of her juvenalia and her only novel. "She did not wish to be discovered," wrote Nigel Nicolson, the British man of letters, "which feeds our longing to discover her." The same might be said of Fanny Holmes.

NOTES ON FANNY

[1] Brigadier General Frederick W. Lander at the time of the battle of Ball's Bluff commanded a brigade in General Stone's Corps of Observation.

[2] Catherine Drinker Bowen, *Yankee from Olympus*, p. 158.

[3] Francis Biddle, *A Casual Past* (Garden City, N.Y.: Doubleday & Company, Inc., 1961) p. 282.

[4] William James (1842–1910), contemporary and close friend of Wendell, most widely read American philosopher of the 1900s. Author of *The Will to Believe* and *Varieties of Religious Experience*. Brother of Henry James, the novelist.

[5] Phillips Brooks (1835–1893), noted American Episcopal clergyman and bishop. Author of "O Little Town of Bethlehem." The Holmeses' wedding was unusual in that the venue was Episcopal, but the principals were Unitarian.

[6] Thomas Hobbes (1588–1679), English philosopher whose thinking greatly influenced Wendell. Hobbes argued that men are moved by selfish considerations and by fear of others. *Leviathan* was his great work.

[7] Immanuel Kant (1724–1804), German philosopher who wrote the *Critique of Pure Reason*. He answered Hume on generalization, wrote on esthetics and ethics and established the main lines for philosophic development since his day.

[8] John Davis Long (1838–1915), governor of Massachusetts (1880–1882), member of Congress (1883–1889), secretary of the navy under McKinley (1897–1902), and T. R. Republican.

[9] Howe, *The Proving Years*, p. 254.

[10] Boston *Daily Advertiser*, April 19, 1880, p. 2; *Nation* 32:286 (April 21, 1881); *The American Architect and Building News*, 9:210, 211 (April 30, 1881).

[11] Howe, *The Proving Years*, pp. 96 et seq.

[12] See Shakespeare, *Macbeth*. act 3, sc. 4, line 24.

[13] (Christopher) Grant La Farge (1862–1938), architect, designer of Saint Matthew's Cathedral in Washington.

[14] Wister, *Roosevelt*, p. 128.

[15] Richard Walden Hale, *Some Table Talk of Justice Holmes and "The Mrs."* Boston, 1935, p. 6. (privately published)

[16] William Jennings Bryan (1860–1925), lawyer, editor, fabulous orator who won fame for his "Cross of Gold" speech at the Democratic Convention in 1896. Three times unsuccessful Democratic candidate for the presidency.

[17] (Thomas) Woodrow Wilson (1856–1924), Princeton professor, writer on political and constitutional matters, president of Princeton, governor of New Jersey and twenty-eighth president of the United States.

[18] William Rufus Day (1849–1923), secretary of state; chairman of commission to arrange peace with Spain, associate justice, U.S. Supreme Court (1903–23).

MISTRESS OF DONERAILE. *The Honorable Emily Ursula Clare (St. Leger) Fitzpatrick, Lady Castletown, wife of the Baron of Upper Ossory and warm friend of Wendell.*

[19] Biddle, *A Casual Past*, p. 289.

[20] Mrs. James B. Ayer, letter to Mark DeWolfe Howe, October 25, 1955, in Howe file in Harvard Law School Library.

[21] Mrs. John G. Palfrey, wife of Wendell's lawyer, mother of world-class tennis player, Sarah Palfrey, who was a three-time winner of the U.S. women's doubles championship and the winner of the women's singles (from Helen Jacobs) in 1945.

[22] Hale, *Table Talk*, p. 9.

[23] Biddle, *Mr. Justice Holmes*, p. 151.

[24] The *Greek Anthology* is a collection of short Greek poems for the most part in elegiac meter and the immediate epigram was written by Theodoridas, a Syracusan poet of the second half of the third century B.C., *The Greek Anthology*, Harvard University Press, book 7, vol. 2, p. 155.

[25] H(orace) Chapman Rose (1907–   ), secretary to Wendell (1931–32), Assistant Secretary of the Treasury (1953–55), Under Secretary of the Treasury (1955–56), partner, Jones Day Reavis & Pogue.

The Dames

Wendell's relationships with women were a central element in his life, and the extent and character of these associations have puzzled and intrigued his biographers. His mother and his wife, as might be expected, played important roles, but their significance was greater than is ordinarily the case in such relations. A warm and tender affection between Wendell and his mother shines forth in the Civil War letters which he preserved. In addition, they shared a similarity of disposition, which included a strain of melancholy and contrasted sharply with the bright extroversion of Dr. Holmes. In Wendell's younger years, his mother gave him the sense of security which was so important to one of his temperament. In Wendell's later years, this stability was provided by Fanny, who added a strong sense of purpose and a firmness of decision.

Beside these expectable attachments, Wendell sought association with a variety of sympathetic and attractive women. As with Woodrow Wilson (a comparison he would have hated), there was an element in Wendell's nature that loved the sparkle and challenge of female companionship, welcomed the opportunity to dramatize himself with the opposite sex, and found satisfaction in their admiration and approval. This attraction was constant—from his days as a returning war hero in Boston to his last years when he took pretty girls on auto rides in the Virginia countryside.

Wendell told Isabella Wigglesworth, wife of Fanny's nephew, that he "loved the dames." She described her first meeting with him:

> I had just become engaged to Aunt Fanny's nephew, Frank, and I was taken over to call on them at Beverly Farms. I was about twenty years old and very green. Aunt Fanny was there when I arrived and she said, "Oh, Wendell's asleep upstairs." So, she went and got a cane out of the umbrella stand and pounded on the ceiling to wake him up. Pretty soon, he appeared, looked at

me, gave me a resounding smack and said, "And now, my dear, who are you?"

If Wendell loved the dames, the dames also loved him. His fascination with them began as he convalesced from his war wounds in his father's house on Beacon Street. When the garrulous doctor rushed to publicize the military exploits of the young officer in a magazine article, waves of attractive young women came to pay homage. As he grew older, this attraction continued as his fame widened, his physical appearance became more impressive, and his charm matured.

Referring to Wendell when he was in his late seventies, Katharine Bundy asserted, "He loved the ladies. He adored adulation and his tea parties were such fun because, as he said, 'the proper geese have left the proper ganders to come and play with the old man.'" Included in his group of intimates were: Frances Noyes, Mrs. LaRue Brown, Ellen Shipman, and Sophie Mason. Frances Noyes, the daughter of Newbold Noyes, the proprietor of the *Washington Star,* was the woman he cared for most. She wrote a book about the Hall-Mills murder case and a mystery called *Hide in the Dark.*

In Boston, Mrs. Charles P. Curtis had been a particularly close friend and another intimate was the widow of Senator Albert J. Beveridge. Wendell also carried on an extensive correspondence with interesting ladies whom he had met abroad, such as Baroness Moncheur, Alice Stopford Green, the Irish political activist and wife of the historian, John Richard Green, author of the *History of the English People,* and the marchioness of Tweeddale, the stepdaughter of Lewis Einstein, the American diplomat.

Wendell adopted a breezy and affectionate style in writing to these ladies. In a letter dated March 26, 1919, he told Mrs. Green: "Your letters always make me walk on air even if I do know you have a dear Irish tongue in your head."

On May 6, 1925, he wrote to the Marchioness: "I have vivid thoughts and affectionate recollections of you," and on April 4, 1931: "I wrote because of the vividness of my feeling for you."

On April 5, 1913, he wrote to Mrs. Green about a prospective trip to Europe and her invitation to stay at her house in England:

I can't imagine anything more charming than to walk in your house and look out upon the Thames—but the hitch is here. If I come over this summer and get Fanny to come with me she would anxiously avoid social encounters of every kind. . . . If it should turn out that I came without her, which I am very unwilling to do but she wants me to on the ground that seeing a lot of new people does me as much good as it gives trouble to her. . . . I don't dare contemplate it as yet. I am not so sure, if I did, that it wouldn't be better for me to take rooms. It was enchanting to stay at the Abbey Gardens but I had many misgivings afterwards whether I ought to have done it. I know, my dear, that your welcome would be (ill.) arriére pensée—but still I should worry and so probably ought not do more than be with you for a few days at most. . . .

He loved to joust and banter with clever women, joining them in intimate sessions over tea or lunch and the question persists as to how far these intimacies extended. Some spoke of his "flitting." Others referred to his "ladies over on Beacon Street." One alluded to his "many affairs," asserting that many a Boston woman "thought she was the Justice's girl." Biddle states that Wendell's "innocent blandishments" in Boston made Fanny "suffer not a little." To be sure, in his bachelor days, Wendell, in a letter to William James, quoted by Bowen in *Yankee from Olympus,* wrote: "There are not infrequent times when a bottle of wine, a good dinner, a girl of some trivial sort can fill the hour for me." But somehow, this language smells of the lamp and seems too theatrical to be other than posturing.

Biddle considered that to Wendell, "women were conduits for the expression of masculine egotism" and raised with Bowen the question whether Wendell "would rather kiss a woman's hand than kiss a woman."[1] In other words, was he, as a lady once said of George Moore, the Irish writer, "one who told but did not kiss"? Bowen answered that she "never understood that side of him," that it was "distasteful to her" and that "it would have been so much easier to understand a passionate man who sins, weeps, is forgiven—and then repeats the process. . . ." His dallying even caused some to wonder whether he was physically capable of having an affair.

Corcoran, who first knew Wendell when Wendell was eighty-five, characterized stories about him and "women" with an

Anglo-Saxon epithet. Rowe, who came with Wendell when the justice was ninety-three, concluded that in amatory jousting Wendell "talked a good game." However, he conceded that, "he was a ladies' man. He loved the ladies, and they all came, these old ladies came one by one to see him, and some of the young ones he picked up."

"I remember once during the winter—I can still remember it—" Rowe once said, "it was a very cold day, and I was throwing another log on the fire. And I heard the old Judge say, 'Oo-la-la!' And I turned and said, 'What did you say, Mr. Justice?' He said, 'I said Oo-la-la!' And I said, 'Why did you say that?' 'Well,' he said, 'I was remembering walking down the street with a lady, and her husband was ahead of us and we were holding hands behind his back.' That was the end of that. He never said who it was."

Shown a rotogravure section photo of a parade of international bathing beauties, when he was approaching ninety, Wendell, after a close examination of the picture said: "I wouldn't mind toying a leisure hour with Miss Czechoslovakia."

Fanny came to hold a realistic, if somewhat resigned, view of Wendell's susceptibility to women and his naiveté where they were concerned. When one of the Boston ladies had gushingly agreed with his conclusions about a vital social problem, Fanny, according to Bowen, told him that it was easy "to mistake worldliness for wisdom." In perplexed soliloquy, in her book, Bowen made Fanny wonder: "How is it possible to have such depth of intellect, such quickness of spirit, yet remain blind, where women are concerned, to the obvious?"

A Wister anecdote illustrates the humor with which she bore his peccadilloes. Many years before, that author and Senator George Wharton Pepper[2] attended a dinner at which Wendell and Fanny were present. The senator and the author were seated next to her while Wendell was at the other end of the table next to Mrs. Gifford Pinchot,[3] a beautiful, red-haired, young woman. The conversation, which had been extremely animated, suddenly lapsed as Fanny's attention appeared to lag. The younger man offered his apologies. "I hope I haven't bored you, Mrs. Holmes," he said. "Oh, no, no," she said, "I noticed that we're the ranking guests and no one can go home until we go home." She nodded toward the other end of the table. "I've tried to catch Wendell's eye, but have you ever seen

the warthog? The warthog has only one eye and it is a *fierce*
eye. I got the warthog eye in return."

NOTES ON THE DAMES

[1] Biddle: *A Casual Past*, pp. 288–89.

[2] George Wharton Pepper (1867–1961), Philadelphia lawyer, U.S. Senator
(1922–27), author and writer on legal subjects.

[3] Wife of Gifford Pinchot who was an American political leader and con-
servationist, first professional American forester, chief of Forest Service (1898–
1910). Main figure in Pinchot-Ballinger controversy in Taft administration
(1910).

Lady C.

While much of Wendell's flitting with the ladies could be dismissed as harmless posturing, his long and fervid relationship with Lady Clare Castletown must be placed in an entirely different category. Emily Ursula Clare Saint Leger, the daughter of the Fourth Viscount Doneraile, was the wife of Bernard Edward Barnaby Fitzpatrick, Baron Castletown of Upper Ossory. He was a graduate of Eton and Oxford (Brasenose) and had served as a life guards officer, as sheriff of Queen's County and as a member of Parliament for Portarlington. His family estates comprised 22,510 acres in Queen's (now Laois) County, Ireland, with an income before the First World War of £15,758 a year ($850,000 in today's dollars). Although elected as a Conservative, one commentator said of him: "No one except Lord C. himself can, I think, say what his political principles are: I should make even that reservation with reservations."[1] The principal residence of the Castletowns in Ireland was at Grantstown (Granston) in Queen's County, but they lived also at the house of her family, Doneraile Court,[2] situated north of Mallow in Cork County. They also had a house at Chester Square in London.

While Lady Clare possessed wealth and status, it is apparent that the simple pastoral life she was leading and the personality of her husband did not satisfy the needs of her nature. Without children to occupy her attention, she was ripe to be captivated by the handsome and charming visitor from Massachusetts. Her husband loved horseplay, big-game shoots, and wardroom humor. This general knocking about doubtless grew less congenial over the years to a gentler soul who found pleasure in discussing art and literature with a more sympathetic person— such as Wendell, while other guests were shooting or riding to the hounds.

That there was some abnormality in the relations between Clare and her husband, Barney Fitzpatrick, is apparent in his book of memoirs which was published in 1926, the year of her

71

death; the book barely mentions his wife of forty-nine years. Accordingly, her search for sympathetic understanding was not limited, as testified to by "intimate" letters recorded in the Archives Office in London. While she encouraged Wendell's advances, she was a "friend and clearly a lover" of the melo-dramatically named Percy Latouche of Newbery, Kilcullen, County Kildare, Ireland. Clare was just forty-three—and Wendell fifty-five—when they met. He experienced an emotional trauma which rivalled the physical blow of the bullet that had struck him at Ball's Bluff thirty-five years before. She swept him off his feet and the passion and strength of his sentiments surge through the 103 letters he wrote her over the next thirty years—copies of which are on deposit in the Harvard Law School Library. Begun in Cork City, immediately after his departure at the close of his first visit to Doneraile, the corre-spondence continues until the time of her death in 1926 and contains some of the tenderest and most sensuous prose writ-ten by this master of the English language. Some of them rank with the great love letters of all time.

Since none of Lady Castletown's letters survive, the picture created by this correspondence is somewhat one-sided; it leaves the lady as a vague and mysterious figure while revealing in a blaze of light all the intimacies of Wendell's emotional nature. The survival of her letters is all the more significant in view of his efforts to keep the exchange secret. He had her address her letters to him at the Court House in Boston and his letters were frequently written from the same place. With characteristic caution, he admonished her to dispose of his letters. On September 5, 1898, he sent a warning: "By the by permit me to suggest that you do not put my letters into the waste paper basket which you trust so much. Fire or fragments and the waterways when you destroy if you do as I do."

From the very beginning of the correspondence, it is appar-ent that Lady Castletown had set profound vibrations in mo-tion. Wendell's first letter was written at 8:00 P.M., the evening of his departure from Doneraile, on August 22, 1896, on sta-tionery of The Queen's Hotel in Queenstown (now Cobh), some forty miles away, where he had gone to take the boat to Boston.

> My dear Lady,
>   It is the stopping so sudden that hurts as your countryman

truly remarked. I am here. I have eaten my dinner without heart and my only amusement is to imagine just how far you have got with your new pleasures. I saw them getting into the vehicle and I approve your judgment.

I forgot to steal some notepaper and I can't write with this pen. I only cling to your hand for a moment until the earth puts its shoulder between us—which is more than the world can do I hope in twenty years. Goodbye dear friend goodbye, my heart aches to think how long it may be.

Yours always
O. W. Holmes.

The Lady Castletown.

Please follow me with a line before I get home I shall so long to hear from you.

Hon. O. W. H.
Court House,
Boston

The next letter, written on the stationery of the Cunard Royal Steamship *Etruria* was begun on the next day, Sunday, August 23, 1896, and contained entries for subsequent days, constituting a mini-journal of the trip as well as a *cri du coeur*.

My dear Lady,

I sent you a line of farewell last and now am well out to sea. But still I can't break off. There are so many things I should have said but only thought of too late. And yet when you get this the telegrapher will be in the ascendant once more. Ah well, I also am one having authority - (Do you think the cheek of that, how horrid?)

24th. Last night I talked with an old Catholic priest who united with me in the odious vice of smoking. I talked with him because he came aboard with me from Queenstown and he seemed to keep me a little nearer to Hibernia. It is a gray morning with a leaden sea and I too am somewhat leaden—not from the sea—You are reading my Queenstown letter. . . .

25th. The farther I get away the harder does it seem. Meantime I imagine the divertissements of Doneraile continuing and am not the more unselfishly happy on that account.

26th. A distraction and a misery. I am nailed to preside at one of these infernal concerts in aid of whatever they do aid. If I try to think of something to say I shall not have to think of you.

27th. Yesterday was, and to-day begins, under the shadow of their hellish entertainment—but I sit and meditate about you and when I ought to be preparing a speech. The speech will be a poor thing in consequence and you none the happier unless you tell me that this makes you so. If, as I asked you, you have written to me don't answer this unless you want to wait for my answer—so will a regular course be established—but write you must. No one sees your letters and they shall be destroyed if you prefer. . . .

The feigned irritation at his shipboard role is characteristic of Wendell, but the impression and ambiguity of his observations accompanied a troubled incoherence that is not characteristic. This is not the calm Olympian of the letters to Pollock or Laski.

Wendell received the letter which he awaited so eagerly and responded immediately:

> Commonwealth of Massachusetts,
> Supreme Judicial Court,
> Court House,
> Boston, Saturday Sept. 5/'96.

Dear Lady,

I have just this moment received your most adorable letter. It is what I have been longing for and is water to my thirst. You say and do everything exactly as I should have dreamed. I shall keep it and when I am blue and you seem far away I shall take it out and read it and be happy again. Do I often come back? I love your asking it. I think my letter from shipboard answered for that time and now I answer for since then and hereafter. Oh yes indeed I do and shall. I do not forget easily, believe me—and your letter was all that was wanting to assure me that we should abide together. If you believe that, distance is easily, or at least more easily, borne. I say your letter was all that was wanting to assure me. Possibly one thing more—an assurance that you too do not forget easily when the moment is past. (*Later.* Tell me that for I have been thinking and thinking about it.) If you say it I shall believe it. I still carry in my pocket a handkerchief (one of my own with a little infinitesimal dark smear upon it—with it I once rubbed away a—Do you remember?

Isn't that a fool thing for a serious Judge? . . . By the by, I ordered the second imprint of my speeches to be sent to you as soon as I arrived. Read them again and the 2nd memorial day one which you haven't seen, love them a little, for I put my heart into the accidental occasion—just that is to say to one who cares, you will understand that there is high ambition and an ideal in this externally dull routine and much of the passion of life. . . . I was not able to get to Bev. Farms on my arrival a week ago Saturday. All was prepared to receive me—my nephew of whom I told you has gone and got engaged and he and his young woman were expecting me at 7½ p.m. When the thing was over, my wife, though far from well went to the livery stables for a driver and a pair of horses and posted through the night to Boston, 30 or 40 miles, arriving about 1½ in the morning—would not wake me—but, there she was in the morning. Imagine my joy—but also my shame to have her make the effort rather than myself—although I knew I ought not to do it on the infernal consideration of health which I have to remember all the time. . . .

Well dear lady I must stop for the moment. Write to me soon. I long every day to hear from you, and live Doneraile over—I picture you to myself in all sorts of ways. By and by we shall settle into some sort of rhythm in writing—but I have not yet learned patience in waiting. The thing to believe and take comfort in, however, is that we are not going to part company—and I am very sure that if we do it will not be I who does it—I am only less confident that it will not be you.

H.

The thought of Fanny, far from well, posting through the night over the thirty odd miles to Boston arouses our compassion and there is a slightly hollow ring in Wendell's expression of regret. One may well ask whether it was necessary at all for him to describe to Lady C. this somewhat demeaning exercise of Fanny.

There is great ambiguity in the words "abide together" in their suggestion as to both past and future activity and speculation is stimulated as to the composition of the "dark smear" and its source. One wonders also in what ways he pictured her to himself.

The cryptic signature was one he was to use at various times.

Wendell sent a brief, informal and urgent note prefiguring his later discussion of the permanence of their intimacy and, although undated, it apparently was despatched soon after his letter of September fifth:

Monday 10 a.m.   Court House

It is so hard to stop. Will you remember me when the other amusements begin? as they will if they have not already. The suggestion of p. 77 is of ambiguous import—but you didn't mean it so did you? Which is which from our point of view? How much more we might have talked had I dared assume that you thought our intimacy permanent. I think it so unless you forbid me. At 7 this a.m. which is 12 with you I was awake and thinking of you. Where were you? Answer this soon. I must to work. I know I am forgetting a lot of things I wanted to say but they will come in time.

Goodbye
H.

I open this to add two things—please send me the photographs as soon as may be—also I hate that little colored picture in your scrap book wh. someone gave you of a woman and dog—I *don't* mean the photograph of you.

The reference to "p. 77" is unclear but tantalizing. It seems unlikely that Lady Clare could have written a letter of this length. Perhaps this was the citation of a passage in some book known to both of them, but one is left to wonder where it was and what its import.

Wendell's next full letter was written while on the circuit he had described to Lady C. and its mood is somewhat more settled than that of those preceding it. The judgment of his host city reveals a marked provincialism:

Worcester,
Mass.

Sept. 30/96
Wednesday
7¾ P.M.

Dear Lady

I am here for a few days on circuit (address always Court
House Boston) for one of the hardest weeks of the year—and I
did hope that it would be mitigated by a letter from you. I have
received two—the last Sept. 6 in answer to mine written at sea. I
have written 2 since that and sent you my book. Oh it is time
that I heard. This is only to give you a fillip and to repeat Rip
Van Winkle's are we so soon forgotten when we are dead? Little
things still happen which connect me with Doneraile very
closely in an external way. I don't need them—believe me, but
there is a sort and delight in them. For instance a day or two ago
I put on for the first time the thick boots on which I took my last
walk with you and found them stiff from the wetting of that day
and dull from the oiling they got afterwards. But the moment
you are silent I begin to wonder whether the shadow is getting
dimmed contrary to nature by the intervention of substance?

I am no good for a letter at this moment after law and jaw
from 9 to 6. . . . If a letter or letters of yours don't cross this I
shall think ill of you, but they will. I find your writing adorable—
you talk—and yet we got to know each other and that is much.
How you would hate this town where I am spending a week.
How dull and squalid the whole business and surroundings
would seem—and yet when you put into them that they afford a
chance to do a part of one's work they don't trouble you and
your spirit is as calm as great fatigue will let it be. I shall go back
to my hotel in a moment—play a game of solitaire on my bed,
read a little Hegel and turn in early.

Goodbye—as I said this is put to stir you up—and forbid you
to forget me. I think of you and think and think—and sit in the
conservatory.

H.

Don't forget to send me the
photograph.

Wendell refers to the Doneraile "conservatory"—as he does
more specifically later—as a place holding magical memories
for him.

His next letter was written a week later and makes a significant reference to Fanny, but, while purporting to clarify his feelings about the two ladies, makes even more ambiguous the exact state of his relation to each:

COMMONWEALTH OF MASSACHUSETTS
Supreme Judicial Court,
Court House, Boston.

Thursday a.m.
October 7, 1896.

Dear Literal Lady,

I have received your third letter (Sept 25th recd. last—Two answers begun before this and burned. It didn't matter—the quickest mail closed Friday) It is adorable like its predecessors. I have read them until I learn them. I should think mine are very slow in getting to you. I have written two or three since the one you mentioned—the last from Worcester last week. . . . But you were literal. Does my writing—did my talk sound as if I thought we were casual acquaintances? Such a surmise is a million years in the past. . . . All I meant was to reproduce my first feeling that one cannot assume at once from the fact that one has talked with an open heart that the other is doing more than yielding for a moment to a fancy of the moment and showing an intimacy by which she may not be prepared to abide. We were both very loud in our profession of familiarity with somewhat cynical views of life, but thank the Lord we neither of us are cynical at bottom and my guards are down long ago. I believe you seriously and sincerely and it would be a deep grief to me to dream it possible that any thing could interrupt our affection. My life is my wife and my work but as you see that does not prevent a romantic feeling which it would cut me to the heart to have you repudiate. But why talk like that? You must know me pretty well, and as I said I believe in you. As the little boy said when the other one said 'Give me the core' (of the apple). 'There ain't going to be no core'—There ain't going to be no repudiation and I am rather ashamed to have squared off so at you—I won't begin my letter over again but pass to other themes. You speak of the touch of isolation in my speeches. It has reference to my work. One cannot cut a new path as I have tried to do without isolation. I have felt horribly alone. But the result has been far more immediate than I have dared dream of its being and the real danger perhaps is that when one has been for a moment in the lead, he should wrap himself in his solitude and sit down and before he knows it instead of being in advance the procession has passed him and his solitude is in the rear. . . . While you are reading I am sitting in court and writing decisions when you don't break up my work as you are doing now. You have done enough disturbance to please even your imperious demands. I have been dreaming with you when I should have been deciding whether an ambiguous document is a promissory note. . . . I haven't been reading much—mainly a book of Hegel's. The beast has insights, but these are wrapped up in such a humbugging method and with so much that is unintelligible or unreal or both that you have to work your way. . . . Now I am going to call on Lady Playfair an amiable Boston girl and to ask her if she knows you. If she does she will have an excess of what otherwise she has to offer. . . . I send her a bunch of roses when she comes here, and she talks to me about an old friend whom this time I have seen as lately as she. Oh my very dearest friend how I do long to see you. I know your hands reach across the sea and I kiss them. I continually hunger and thirst for letters. But oh if I could see you. Au revoir.

H.

In differentiating between the objects of his affection, Wendell shows a scholastic capacity to distinguish when he says that his life is equally in his "wife" and his "work"—but that he can still harbor a "romantic feeling" for the new object of his affections. How far from a true understanding of the judicial mind, one speculates, must have been those advocates in the Boston Court House arguing before him the ambiguities of an alleged promissory note. Here, too, Wendell seizes the opportunity, offered him by Lady Clare, to picture himself as the romantically lone mariner navigating for the first time seas of thought which no other has previously sailed.

In a letter written at the beginning of the week after the national election—the outcome of which he appears to have miscalculated—Wendell figuratively rides the range of subjects:

Monday a.m.
November 9, 1896.

I was disappointed on Saturday not to get a letter from you—and lo and behold, this morning I get a perfectly dear one which makes me happy, when I was blue, and has given me as much of a start as McKinley's election has given the country. Really I am not expressing in cold words the delight I feel. Understand it— also I loved your [?] at one place in the letter. As Lord Coke says Littleton's 'etc.' covered a multitude of nice points. . . . It is quite sure that I do want a tremendous lot of your sympathy and I never doubt that you would give it to me in all the serious interests of my work if I had the chance to explain all that I was thinking about from moment to moment. I take all for granted dear friend as I hope and believe you do. At the same time I want you to keep telling me of it until the air hums. *Please* don't let it be so long again. What a dreadful thing distance is. . . . I have just read two improper French books—one light wicked and amusing—the other serious and rather [?]. The latter (Aphrodite) led me to reflect for the 10000000000th time on the illusion of freedom. A man says I am going to let myself slip and have my heart out—and he finds that out of restraint he got an infinity by suggestion which vanishes before the finite act. I told my wife, a propos, that morals were like an intelligent French stage dress which by partial concealment effects an indecency that one would vainly strive for with the nude. You must keep one stocking on if you want a figure to look undressed. . . .

After intervening letters, a hasty line from Wendell expresses his exasperation that the demands of the workaday world tear him from extended communication with his "dear lady."

> Friday
> December 4/96
> 1 PM

My Dear Lady

A letter from you, ah so short and hurried, has come this minute—and the mail closes at 3 and I have much that must be done meantime, but I will send you a line (I am interrupted by a notice that a Congressman whom I invited to lunch is waiting for me—and for you)—a line to kiss your dear hands—and to tell you that you are mistress of the troublant in your discourse—by Jove—but I long to see you.

I will write soon—but you dont deserve it for you might take more trouble for a fellow.

Remember me meantime amid your diversions.

> Yours ever
> OWH

The modern reader irrelevantly feels a twinge of nostalgia at the confidence of the writer in the punctual performance of the postal service. The politically sensitive is intrigued by Wendell's seeking out a member of Congress for lunch—a mundane relationship of a type rarely mentioned in his letters—and wonders if the conference may have had some relationship to the recent election which will transfer administration of the government in Washington to members of Wendell's party. A student of Wendell's *tendresse* will note his fascination with the kissing of hands as well as his expression of permanent dedication at the close.

Later that same day after the congressional lunch, and repentant over the brevity of this note, Wendell wrote a longer and less harried reply to Lady C.

Following several previous letters and inspired by a particularly warm missive from Lady Clare, Wendell (on February 2, 1897) soared into an emotional response, tempered, however, by a longish but colorful critique of the French novels he had been reading.

There is no salutation this time:

> Yesterday as I hoped I received one from you marked Jan. 23 that thrilled me through and through. The sadness, the passionate eloquence and the ever elusive shimmer of it, which you command so well, I loved them all. Were you thinking of some past I know nothing about or the present I wonder, with a man's sceptical stupid tenderly solicitous mind. Adorable exasperating gift of the little joker—now you see it and now you don't. I saw *you* at all events as I always long to see you and it makes me happy when I do. I shall send you by this mail the photograph I had taken for you as I wrote the other day. . . . I had it green for Ireland. I hope you will like it. You will see that I am looking at you as you bid me do—and I was thinking of you in the conservatory, I believe, so far as it is possible to think of anything after being emptied of all content by the glare and the fussy manipulation of the photographer. . . . Tell me when you receive it and if it is all right so that I can have the negative destroyed.
>
> I have been reading P. Loti's *Galilée*.[3] I took it up some time ago but dropped it and now have taken it up again and finished it. *Pêcheur d'Islande* for the first time makes articulate the sense of the antediluvian. What I have often tried to describe as I realized it coming down the [?] to the top of the [?] Glacier[4]

where one seems to have got behind the scenes into the workshop of creation—where behemoth was made—where man was not expected and it was sacrilege to go. Then *Au Maroc* gives you a similar feeling about man—the feeling that I got looking at the photograph of the Pharaoh—and thinking that there was the actual part of one who stood on the arrete at the top of all the recorded self knowledge of the race, that is, at the beginning of History—and looking back at the ascent on the other side—the feeling that it gives me to think that a hundred and fifty successive men, who could be gathered in a small room, take us back to the unknown. . . .—*Galilée* is something of the same with the figure of Christ *living* in it for a moment. Yet I suspect his thought to be rather banal—and that his gift is his amazing power of description of which he makes the 19th cent. cocktail—bitter, sweet, hot, cold, strong. As Jules Lemaitre[5] says, he likes Renan,[6] though, for a different combination he is *troublant*—in Renan it is the union of passion or rather enthusiasm and irony, both equally genuine. In P.L. it is the *primitif* and the *affiné*. I kiss your hands . . . I met my philanthropic cousin last night and asked her why she didn't send me the improving article on Charities which she promised me for you. I wish I knew more definitely why you are always sad. Women are more often so than men, I think. They have more time to think at large and apart from the matter in hands. I can't stop to sympathize with the sorrows of the race even if I were not bitterly conscious that I do not love my fellowman as much as I ought. But I infer that with you it is more specified. I have some things to feel sad about. For one my old partner, with whom I studied, and to whom I am bound by a thousand ties, is very ill—a great head, a strong heart and a mighty energy—Yet I am such a damned egotist, I am so full of my work, so eager to prove my power— that I get the fundamental vital happiness out of life in spite of everything. I should think better of myself if I were more miserable. Goodbye. You are very dear.

O.W.H.

Regardless of his balancing of his initial surge of emotion with a more detached intellectual commentary, he makes plain the profundity of his feeling and the continuing strength of his commitment. Further quotation is not required to demonstrate that this attachment was powerful and not an ephemeral fancy.

Since the quoted letters provide an adequate picture of Wendell's mind and emotions, it is appropriate to pass over numer-

numerous other letters written in this period and jump to correspondence regarding his plans for a second visit to Lady Clare—a matter over which he fussed and fretted and to which he devoted a great deal of time and thought. Early in the vital year, he began to hash over the details of his trip, greeting his friend with a more intimate, if somewhat arch, Celtic cognomen:

COMMONWEALTH OF MASSACHUSETTS
Supreme Judicial Court,
Court House, Boston

February 17, 1898.

Dear Hibernia,

You have the gift of graces and the gift of charm when you see fit to use them—that I swear. I can't tell you how the few words of your wire pleased me, apart from the weight they lifted off my mind. And it was a weight. Now I have received a second letter which shows that the burden has begun to lift a little from you even then. I proceed to answer that, I have very little doubt that I shall come over this summer unless something goes wrong unexpectedly. Unfortunately I cannot choose my time. . . . As my time is so short, and I have a good many friends and acquaintances in England I would rather not be torn by you going to France until I had left, especially as I have to be careful still. I loathe the idea of your finding another playmate however. You will do what you can to help me see as much of you as possible wont you? I imagine all sorts of adorable romantic visits or excursions, such as England is full of—and some one or more of which it seems as if our [?]—even a hansom in London is an enchanted solitude. But indeed there will be enchantment wherever I see you and when I think of it with any realizing feeling my heart stands still. Would you dine with me some evg? Several people did, last time. You would smile if you saw some of my learned friends but I am not sure that I ought not to make more of a point of seeing the remarkable men who know anything I am interested in than I did the last time. I used to say that the common or garden judge didn't fizzle and that I would rather talk to a nice girl. Perhaps if I had been less interested in talking to nice girls it wd. have been better for my reputation, considered as an article to be helped or hurt by conduct. But I always have neglected it in that way, and have contented myself with grinding my teeth and raging inwardly when I heard the second

rate exalted and talked of in terms of the 1st rate and when I
heard myself talked of in any terms by people who didn't understand my aims and my ideas on the plane on which I talked—so
there—laugh again at my egotism if you like. By the way I do
despise the apologetic *"Egoism"* without the T which is in
common use nowadays. Now then quick my charmeress tell me
that something nice will be practical within the times I name. I
have been working pretty hard for three weeks and went home
with a headache yesterday. To-day there is a lull and I have
caught up with my work. Hence I have skipped from the bench
into the adjoining room where being alone I kneel gallantly on
one knee and kiss your beloved hands. . . .

Wendell's concern about being "careful still" seizes the attention. Does this mean that the secrecy of their attachment
would be endangered if they met outside the normal channels
of society in England? Is this inconsistent with his visions of
"romantic excursions"? Does he envisage a time when for
some reason he will no longer have to be careful?

That visits might be both adorable and romantic suggests a
wide range of possible experiences, but one is brought up short
by the tremulous inquiry which indicates that dinner together
would be the peak of bliss and achievement.

His eager imagination could even make a Victorian hansom
a place of enchantment, although its practical limitations as a
place for serious dalliance are readily apparent.

Parenthetically, in this letter Wendell intrudes his constant
and hypersensitive concern about being given his proper due as
a first-rank figure in the world of thought; he demonstrates his
almost petty concern about the niceties of language with his
stricture on the use of *egoism,* an indulgence which his opposition has not affected.

After three other letters, Wendell wrote briefly, showing his
anxiety about their meeting and his concern that his letters
should not be seen by those who might not understand—or
who might understand too well:

March 18/98

Dear Hibernia,
    This is just to say that I despatched a letter to you—"British
Legation, Tangier, Morocco." If by any chance you are not
there perhaps it were as well to send for it. Until I have reopened

communication I hesitate to write freely. I shall wait anxiously for an answer to my inquiries whether your last letter meant that there was any, the slightest doubt of my seeing you *somewhere.* I have assumed that you would make an effort if one were necessary—I need not say that I would.

The spring is in the air and you are in my heart.

I kyh,
O.W.H.

Wendell was a fidgety swain indeed. After the certainty he had already expressed about his plans, as the time for sailing approached, he broke out in a rash of scruples and doubts. Conceivably Fanny's physical condition might have been a factor. She had suffered through a long siege of rheumatic fever in 1896; its effects were debilitating and her recovery slow. To be sure, Wendell did not mention this:

June 9/98

Beloved friend. I am nigh insane with the question of coming to England. I had made up my mind that I ought to put it off and my wife now urges me to go and threatens horrid results to me if I do not. I feel I shall be a selfish pig if I do, and I don't know. If I do not come yõu will know that I do not give up seeing you even for a time—i.e. put it off a year without deep sorrow. Since I began to write I have almost decided not to come. I will not go into the reasons which really amount to a delicate balancing of what is the fair thing etc. under existing circumstances—but I do entreat you neither to scold nor to turn away in vexation. I really believe that it disappoints me even more than I hope it will you—and that is a good deal. If I have entered into your life hold fast to me even though it has to be with a hand (I kiss it) stretched across the Atlantic. Life seems short and its chances few. One thing that tremendously urges me to go is the reflection that I am sur le retour[7] and opportunities are not to be trifled with. Next year I shall hope to come—for if that were disappointed also—the next I am anchored with the summer equity. Oh my friend how will it be? Shall I get a cross answer or one of those in which you let out your adorable kindness?

Of course something still may happen to change my mind—but I regard it as definitely less likely than it has been hereto fore.

Yours
OWH

It is impossible to escape the feeling that Wendell enjoyed this Hamlet-like soliloquy. Perhaps he was showing the characteristic that the astute Fanny years later was to encapsulate for Felix Frankfurter. "Wendell has a new toy," she told Felix when he came calling and entered their presence in an atmosphere weighted with gloom, "it is called *despair.*"

Then, eleven days later, the clouds dissipated, the sun shone forth and all was well:

POST OFFICE TELEGRAPHS

Ju 18, 98
6:37 p.m.

Boston

TO Lady Castletown   Seventyeight
Chester Sq. Ldn

Just settled sail Umbria June twentyeight

Justice

And so the die was finally cast and, apparently with Fanny's concurrence, "Justice" did sail on the *Umbria,* did reach London seven days later, and did meet his "Hibernia" again after a separation of two years. One cannot help speculating how differently this affair might have been conducted in the present day with its daily jet plane service between Boston and London or Shannon. At the very least, there undoubtedly would have been far fewer than five score letters.

The details of Wendell's visit are sparse. He did meet friends and people of stature in London as he had planned. He did visit Ireland and did spend some time with Lady Clare. Whether or not they were able to enjoy adorable and romantic excursions can only be inferred from a letter he wrote immediately upon his return, which describes not only his profound emotional experience, but also the physical and nervous near-collapse which he suffered. Significantly, even in the midst of prostration, he continued his admonition about the destination of any letters:

BEVERLY FARMS Address Court House
Boston
Sept. 5/98

I am here in the kind of collapse that comes after nervous
tension. The weather is very hot and I suppose I still am relaxed
by the opiate I took the first night. My trouble turned out to be
shingles which accounts for the neuralgia etc. It is getting better
but I still can't sleep through even 6 or 7 hours without a dose.
So don't mind beloved friend if I am dull this time. I hope my
voyage letter caught the return steamer so that you will get it by
the end of this week. I think you will see from it how I yearn and
long for you. Your telegram met me and gave me a joy which I
can't express—only I did so wish that I had found some expression as you did which I could entrust to the telegraph. I
loved your "tender" and hugged it to my heart. And now do you
think you can meet time and distractions and still care for me so
much? I believe you will. I firmly believe that time will make no
difference to me. Oh my dear what a joy it is to feel the inner
chambers of one's soul open for the other to walk in and out at
will. It was just beginning with you. Do not cut it off because of a
little salt water. . . . [Here Wendell issues the warning about
destroying letters which has already been quoted] . . . As I talk
literature dear Clare I kiss your feet and proceed to talk on. It is
rather odd to read letters of Sir W. Knollys[8] to his sister, saying
how much he would like to make many a mother if his existing
encumbrances only might be gathered away, as he had a lawful
lady. . . . This is only a bulletin to repeat my love to you and tell
you how I am.

Yours
H

This is an amazingly revealing epistle. Perhaps the "voyage
letter," being closer to the experience, would have contained
more intimate details of their relations, but, no letter with the
requisite date or context is included in the Harvard collection.
In any case, there is ample material in the foregoing communi-
qué to reemphasize the depth of the passion Wendell had
conceived and made apparent in previous letters and which, we
must conclude, was encouraged and reciprocated by Lady
Clare.

Wendell acknowledges that he belongs to Clare. Abandoning

any formal salutation, he details the "nervous tension" consequent upon their meeting and describes in sensual language their still-expanding intimacy. Even in the course of expressing his deep emotion, his caution asserts itself and he immediately turns to his warning about the destruction of the papers. Of all the revelations, the most significant is found in the reference— after figuratively kissing the feet of "dear Clare"—to the desire of Sir W. Knollys to propagate widely if his existing "encumbrances" could be "gathered away." With Knollys, as with Wendell, there was an existing wife. When Wendell closed by repeating his "love," the word was manifestly not used euphemistically.

The last letter to Lady Clare is dated August 27, 1926; the final letter in this remarkable collection, written on stationery of the Supreme Court of the United States, is dated November 3, 1926, and is directed to Lord Castletown:

My dear Castletown

Please accept my thanks for your kind letter which relieves my wonder but increases my anxiety as to Lady Castletown. I feared but did not know that she was ill. As I do not know the nature of the illness I can do nothing but hope it is not grave. Please give her my love and tell her I think about her a great deal and shall continue anxious until I hear more, & I hope better news. All goes well with me in spite of my 85 years, and I have been hard at work since the October term began—now relieved by three weeks adjournment with all my work done.

With regard to publishers I am rather helpless. From the very little I know I should think G. P. Putnam & Sons New York would be as likely as any that I know of to be interested in your work. Mr. George Haven Putnam[9] who, I suppose, is the head of the firm, is an old soldier of the Civil War and has published reminiscences himself. I have an impression that he is rather in that line. A brother is head of the Library of Congress from which I first got your book before I got a copy for myself. I wish I could tell you more.

You do not say how you are yourself, but I infer that you are well.

Ever sincerely yours
O.W. Holmes

Lady Castletown died on March 11, 1927.
Aside from the last letter to Lord Castletown, there are 102

letters from Wendell to Lady Clare in the Holmes papers at the Harvard Law School Library. A letter or two may have been lost or abstracted, but, barring these, the collection forms a record of his communications over a period of thirty years. Her letters were destroyed by him—although a single cryptic note in the Frankfurter papers at the Library of Congress, reading "O.W.H. Lady Castleton [*sic*], Ireland" suggests that a letter or a photograph might have been removed.

Wendell wrote warm letters to many lady friends. He wrote 330 to Mrs. John Chipman Gray.[10] On occasion, too, he verbally "kissed a lady's hand," but in none of the other series did the passion and sensual imagery kindle the pages as in the letters to Lady Clare. In them there is a unique sense of wonder and of delight.

Although the correspondence covered a period of thirty years, eighty-six letters, or 83 percent of the total, were written in the three years from Wendell's first meeting in 1896 to the period surrounding his second meeting in 1898. Apart from flurries in 1914 and 1916, these were the major years. He wrote eighteen in 1896, including two on December fourth; thirty-three in 1897, including five in December, and thirty-five in 1898, including four and a cable in June prior to his voyage. After 1898, there was a sudden drop in numbers—to two for the year—and then a long hiatus when no letters were sent, from that year until 1914. The letters were then resumed, but they had become more impersonal and detached.

Several possible reasons explain this change of direction. For one thing, Wendell became Chief Justice of the Massachusetts Supreme Judicial Court in 1899 and this promotion altered his obligations and way of life and restricted his freedom. For another, he and Lady Clare may have realized the difficulties that lay in the way of any change of their relationship. Finally, there is a strong suspicion that Fanny, knowing Wendell better than he knew himself, put her foot down, as she was supremely able to do.

Wendell made several other visits to the home of the Castletowns at Doneraile Court in Cork County. He stayed there in 1903 after he had gone on the bench of the Supreme Court of the United States. At that time he made the acquaintance of the Anglicized Irish novelist and Roman Catholic canon, Patrick Augustine Sheehan, a friend of the Castletowns and pastor of the Doneraile parish church. This acquaintance ripened into a warm friendship and resulted in a charming exchange of letters (later discussed herein) which have recently been published. Wendell visited Ireland again in 1907 and he saw the Castletowns in 1909 as he "flitted through London" on his way to receive an honorary degree of Doctor of Laws (D.C.L.) at Oxford. His last visit came in 1913, just before the first World War made steamship travel inadvisable.

By this time, the Castletowns had come upon hard times. The fall involved disastrous speculation, loss of property interests, receivership, vastly reduced income, physical decline for Lord Castletown and a painful eye operation for Lady Clare. Canon Sheehan told Wendell in March 1911 that Doneraile Court had had to be let and that the deer in the park had been killed and their meat sold. He added that "universal sympathy" had been "awakened for Lord and Lady Castletown, especially the latter." But conditions proved to be somewhat better than the canon had feared; Wendell was entertained in adequate style when, after again fussing about traveling without Fanny, he went on to Doneraile after "the season" in London had ended.

Canon Sheehan died later in the same year. It is interesting to note that at no time during his ten-year friendship with Wendell did this Catholic pastor give any indication that he felt the intentions of his American friend toward Her Ladyship were anything other than strictly honorable.

In view of the warmth of the relations between Wendell and Lady Clare and the extent of their correspondence, it is somewhat strange that this remarkable romantic excursion has never come to light. There are only the briefest of references to the Castletowns in the major compilations of letters and biographies and the existence of this fascinating collection appears to be known to very few people. In fact, the existence of the letters was not known until Mark Howe, working on the authorized biography of Wendell and coming upon the Castletown connection, concluded that letters must have survived. Advised by his wife, Molly (herself Irish, a novelist and former Abbey Theatre actress), he found a Joycean, Dublin character to investigate. This was Eoin "Pope" O'Mahoney, a feckless geneologist and descendant of Daniel O'Connell, the Irish Liberator. The sobriquet had been bestowed on O'Mahoney because of his exalted rank in the Knights of Malta, a Catholic order given to gorgeous uniforms and dedicated to the defense of the Papacy. O'Mahoney went down to Cork and discovered that, contrary to Wendell's direction, his letters had not been destroyed. They were in the possession of the latter day Lady Doneraile whose husband was a distant cousin of Lady Clare. Handwritten copies and typewritten transcripts of the letters were made and these were presented in 1967 by Lady Doneraile to the Harvard Law School Library. The present location of the original letters is not known, although one turns up from time to time in the hands of autograph dealers. A very recent investigation in this country and in Ireland indicated that Mary Lady Doneraile had died in 1975 and that the Doneraile title had lapsed.

Unfortunately, Mark Howe died in 1967 before he had completed the section of his biography dealing with the years of Wendell's acquaintance with Lady Clare. Since Howe's death, thirty years after that of Wendell, other judicial luminaries from Harvard and elsewhere have come to prominence and the keenness of interest in Wendell whom Justice Benjamin N. Cardozo praised so unstintingly has naturally diminished. Symbolically, the great Hopkinson portrait of Wendell has been removed from its prominent, designated place in the main reading room of the Harvard Law School Library and has been relegated to a less notable location in the dim light of a lower floor in Pound Hall. The work which Howe began was never finished, although selected scholars were authorized to continue the task. Thus, the attention of researchers has not been called to this treasure trove and no publication has been made until recently. One might conclude that fate intervened to keep secret this Celtic interlude of Wendell and Lady Clare.

The Castletown affair presents a piquant puzzle. At this late date, what appraisal can be made? How far did it go, and did Fanny know about it?

If the letters had been written in our time, the conclusion that there had been a fully realized relation with physical intimacy would be irresistible. Supporting this conclusion, in the actual case, are the intense and sustained emotional involvement, the supersecrecy and destruction of the evidence suggesting guilt, the pitch and fervor of the language with its images of carnal conjunction, the proposals for romantic excursions, the tendency to extracurricular high jinks in some of the

LADY C. AND WENDELL AT DONERAILE COURT. A walk in the grounds of the Castletown chateau in County Cork as reconstructed from several photographs by artist Jamie Hogan.

British country houses of that day and, finally, the reference Wendell made in one of the letters to Fanny's being an encumbrance to wider ranging on his part.

But, there is another side. We note Wendell's emphasis on symbols of minor substance: the handkerchief with its smudge (of what?), the conservatory, an unlikely place for anything but a furtive squeeze; the excessive use of the figure of kissing a hand (which Wendell used frequently to other correspondents) or, on occasion, the feet, but a complete lack of the specifics of more intimate amorous dalliance, the suggestion of a *diner á deux* as the summit of daring misconduct. If Wendell's attitude toward war was Arthurian, perhaps his attitude toward love was Tennysonian and, as a latter-day Galahad, he kept his passion within bounds. It does appear, however, that his own evidence points in the other direction.

It is worthy of note that Wendell went out of his way with at least three people—Biddle, Corcoran, and Isabella Wigglesworth—to emphasize that he had never been unfaithful to his wife. "I've always liked the dames," he told Wigglesworth, "but I've never stepped over the edge." Was it meaningful that he volunteered this information? Biddle believed him, as did the others, but it appears that Wendell felt the need of a defense and the reiteration raises questions about its reliability.

Fanny was painfully aware of Wendell's tendency to philander, but there is no direct evidence that she knew of the Castletown affair. In estimating what Fanny knew and when she knew it, one is forced to rely upon inferences from the known facts, coupled with a knowledge of Fanny's character, her absorption in him, and her familiarity with his foibles. This story, retold by one of the secretaries, is an example of her technique in dealing with this phenomenon:

"One morning, the Justice had made one of his calls and was being entertained in her home by one of his charming lady friends. After they had settled down and were in the midst of their tête-à-tête, the doorbell rang and a card was brought in. It was Fanny's card and on it was written: 'Wendell, I'm downstairs waiting in the carriage.' Of course, he got up and left immediately."

Both Isabella Wigglesworth and Katharine Bundy, who as younger women knew Fanny, feel certain that she was aware of Lady Clare and Wendell's attraction to her. When asked if she thought that Fanny knew of the correspondence and involvement, Wigglesworth said, "I have been wondering. I bet she did. She was no fool. I bet she urged him to go to see the lady and get it off his chest." Here is a possible and not unreasonable suggestion. Wendell was now fifty-seven and, acting with subtlety and understanding, Fanny pushed the affair to its conclusion. At any rate, the pitch of Wendell's interest in Cork declined markedly and he turned for solace and stimulation to his friends on Beacon Street and in Beverly Farms and to his coterie of devotees in Washington.[11]

NOTES ON LADY C.

[1]G. E. Cokayne, *The Complete Peerage of England, Scotland and Ireland* (London: Gibbs, 1913). The quote is from Rev. A. B. Beavan.

[2]Doneraile Court was one of the Irish "great houses" built by the Anglo-Irish ascendancy and the seat of the Saint Leger family after whom the famous Saint Leger Stakes horse race was named. The surrounding park land has been taken over by the Irish government and the house with its chaste Georgian facade has been donated to and is being restored by the Irish Georgian Society. See *Burke's Guide to Irish Country Houses* (Ireland: Mark Bence-Jones, 1978), vol. 1.

[3]Pierre Loti (Julien Viaud) (1850–1923), naval officer and French novelist; an impressionist writer of penetrating melancholy who excelled in depicting exotic scenes.

[4]Although the descriptive words are illegible in this letter, Wendell was probably repeating a description: "I came down from the Mönch to the top of the Aletsch Glacier and felt as if we were committing a shuddery sacrilege, surprising Nature in her privacy before creation was complete. . . ." Letter to Baroness Moncheur, September 5, 1915. See Howe, *The Shaping Years,* pp. 237, 310.

[5]Jules Francois-Elie Lemaître (1853–1914), French critic and dramatist, member of the Académie français.

[6]Joseph-Ernest Renan (1823–1892), French critic philologist and historian, author of *Vie de Jésus.*

[7]Sur le retour: to be upon the decline of life.

[8]Sir William Thomas Knollys (1797–188s), soldier, treasurer and comptroller of household of the Prince of Wales (1862–77); gentleman usher of the Black Rod (1877–83); father of Viscount Knollys, the letter writer.

[9]George Haven Putnam (1844–1930), president of G. P. Putnam & Son, publishers (1872–1930), served in Union Army through Civil War, organized American Publishers' Copyright League.

[10]Mrs. John Chipman Gray ("Nina") was the wife of the Civil War veteran, lawyer, professor at the Harvard Law School who, uncharacteristically, combined teaching and practice; a close friend of Holmes, for a time Gray chose his secretaries. Author of the once-famous *Rule Against Perpetuities* and *The Nature and Sources of the Law.*

[11]The affair was first publicly treated in John S. Monagan, "The Love Letters of Justice Holmes," *The Boston Globe Magazine,* 24 March 1985, p. 15.

Canon from Cork

Frequent reference has been made to Wendell's geniality, his courtesy and his kindliness, but there are few published examples of his affection and his tenderness. Undoubtedly, his native reticence made him chary of expressing these sentiments, yet they were present in his character and to an impressive degree. In his extensive destruction of his letters, there is no doubt that many evidences of such feelings were removed from the record, yet in the recently published collection of his letters to the Irish priest, Canon Patrick Augustine Sheehan,[1] there appears a tenderness, a sensitivity and a solicitude which he elsewhere purposefully kept from public view. In fact, Wendell was disturbed when he learned that Sheehan's biographer, Herman H. Heuser,[2] possessed copies of these letters which he characterized as having been written "with the freedom one practices to an intimate, expecting no other eyes to see them," but he was pleased with the biography when it was published and considered it a "beautiful memorial."

Patrick Augustine Sheehan was an Irish Roman Catholic priest, eleven years younger than Wendell and the pastor of the parish church in Doneraile, County Cork. The two met there in 1903 while Wendell was visiting his good friend Lady Clare Castletown and her husband at her family home, Doneraile Court. Sheehan was a sensitive and talented man, a lover of literature and a student of the great philosophers, not all of whom were taught in the seminaries. After his ordination, he had spent some time on "the English Mission" where he had acquired an urbanity which made him a welcome intimate in the Castletown house. His Anglicization was such that he shared Lord Castletown's opposition to the Irish Home Rule legislation proposed by the British Liberal government in 1913. David Burton, the editor of *Holmes-Sheehan Correspondence*, has said that the foreign experience in some ways made the Irish priest "an English gentleman-savant." Before having come to Doneraile, some forty miles north of Cork City, Sheehan had been stationed at the cathedral in Queenstown

(Cobh) where he had been given the honorary designation as canon. He had written a half dozen well-received novels of psychological character exploration of which one, *My New Curate,* attained popularity in the United States.

Wendell had met the Castletowns in 1896, but he did not make the acquaintance of the canon until seven years later. And after they had met and entered upon their intimate correspondence with one another, there is no instance where Wendell revealed to Sheehan the depth of his affection for Lady Castletown nor is there any indication that the canon suspected the warmth of Wendell's feeling for his patroness.

Although there were vast philosophical differences between the two men, there also were deep similarities of taste and temperament and the humanity of each bridged the differences and found a mutual sympathy which ripened into warm friendship. They regretted the ocean which separated them and made the opportunities for meeting infrequent. At one point, Wendell wrote: "I wish that we could realize the fable of astral bodies and alternately I sit down with you in your dear well-remembered place and you with me in this library which I think you would like." Nevertheless, the *rapport* which each recognized at their first meeting was broadened and intensified through a wide-ranging correspondence which continued until the canon's death in 1913. In these letters, Sheehan demonstrated a liberality of view unusual among Irish clerics and Wendell a delicacy and lack of inhibition unequalled in his other communications.

After an initial exchange when Wendell sent the canon a volume of his speeches and the latter sent back a copy of one of his books, Wendell made the first disarming and tentative step toward establishing closer relations. On January 2, 1904, he wrote: "I am as far as possible from being on your side—but I still hope you will have room for a little pleasure when I say that your book moves me more intimately by old world feeling than anything that I have read for a great while and that if you did not regard me as an enemy I think it might be that we should recognize each other as friends."[3]

Having finished Sheehan's book of reflections, *Under the Cedars and the Stars,* in February, Wendell wrote again:

"And now I must tell you once more of the love and exaltation which your words have the skill to command, as few words

that I have read anywhere can. It is true that I don't believe
your philosophy—or shall I say, the religion you so beautifully
exalt. . . . But I love an idealist—even while I doubt the cosmic
significance of our judgments."[4]

Sheehan responded promptly with a statement of principle,
remarkable for its tolerance and charity, which must have
moved Wendell deeply:

> Would you let me assure you that there is no antagonism be-
> tween us? We differ in our interpretation of human life and the
> universe around us, but that fact, so far as I am concerned, in no
> wise diminishes my esteem for you. I respect your conscientious
> convictions; nor have I any right to intrude within the sacred
> sanctuary, where each soul is alone with God. Conscience is the
> supreme monitor. I would that all men believed as I do, for I
> believe that this faith is not only the solution of what is other-
> wise inexplicable, but also the great proof and support of the
> human soul under the serious difficulties of life. But I have no
> right to force this conviction on you; and the fact, that you see
> with other eyes than mine, should in no way imperil or diminish
> the friendship, which I take the pleasure of assuming, should
> subsist between us. . . .
>
> I am a great believer in the words of S. Paul: "There remain
> faith, hope and charity; but the greatest of these is charity." I
> have toleration and friendship for all, but one class—the ag-
> gressive and intolerant. . . . We have one supreme obligation—
> to be kind to each other.[5]

Four years later, a greater intimacy is apparent. Wendell,
after having received and partly read a new novel by the canon
writes on March 21, 1908:

"Again, you make me love and admire your tender poetic
idealizing spirit. I received your *Parerga* two days ago and last
night I read the first part, with some little peeps ahead. It is
charming and I am very much obliged to you for sending it to
me. It is strange how little the difference in our point of view
prevents my sympathizing with what seem to me your domi-
nant feelings and attitude."[6]

Wendell does not hesitate from time to time to set forth his
own point of view: ". . . . not to lie awake nights with cosmic
worries—having taken the faith to believe that the world is not
my dream and that I am not running it."

Then with great sensitivity and almost as if abashed by his irreverence, he hastens to add: "Dear Father Sheehan, you don't mind my levities, I hope, knowing the sincerity behind them, a sincerity that includes affection for you."[7]

Again a few years later, in 1910, Wendell, writing as "your heretic friend,"[8] ventures to express doubts as to the validity of a prediction by Father Robert Hugh Benson[9] in the *Atlantic Monthly* that the future belonged to the Catholic Church, but quickly adds almost apologetically:

"You don't mind, I hope, my running on, and popping out with anything that happens to come into my head as I write. Our friendship is sincere enough to excuse reserves that hamper freedom." And he concludes the letter in the same vein: "I send this with some fear that parts of it may strike you as better omitted, but I will take the risk."

Readers of Wendell's other letters will recall the starkness and near-savagery of some of his comments to Harold Laski on similar themes and will appreciate the great tact with which he expresses his thought to Canon Sheehan.

Sheehan rejoices when he can find points of philosophy upon which they can agree as in an observation which Wendell must have smiled to read:

"Would you be surprised to hear that in what you say about 'intellect' you come very near the dogmatic teaching of the Church, especially as revealed in the late Papal Encyclical against 'modernism'—one of the most remarkable documents that has ever been issued by the Holy See?"[10]

At another later point, Wendell characterizes Sheehan's "discourse as to science" as "but a half truth" and continues, "I think science has changed our point of view, and for the better." However, he immediately pulls back, adding "But there I touch controversy."[11]

On April 1, 1911, Wendell wrote to Sheehan setting forth an unusual formulation of views of his that are fundamentally familiar:

Oh my dear Canon you are lonely, but so am I although I am in the world and surrounded by able men—none of those whom I meet has the same interests and emphasis that I do—barring those elements common to all who are trying to solve the same problems and do their duty. I am speaking too only of my work, but that is two thirds of my life. Outside of that my wife has made my whole life a path of beauty. She has a real genius, I say it advisedly and confidently, and has devoted all her powers to surrounding me with enchantments. So that when I say I am lonely, I feel bound to confess that it is egotism—the feeling thrown back on oneself when one sees little attention given to what one thinks most important. I am rather ashamed of my outburst but I shall send my letter as I have written it. The frame of mind that I am afraid I often am in and express is little better than one you would deem sinful. I look at man as a cosmic [insignificance], having neither merit nor demerit except from a human and social point of view, working to some unknown end or no end, outside himself and having sufficient reasons, easily stated, for doing his best.[12]

While the canon was chewing over this statement, he received another communication from Wendell enclosing his "Harvard Speech" of June 1911 which included the assertion that "While we think we are egotists, we are living to ends outside ourselves." Warning Wendell that he had "stirred up the Celt," Sheehan responded,

How cordially I can agree with all this—and yet with what different eyes we look at the same thing and draw different conclusions. I perceive this is what you mean when you say, *Life is painting a picture*. But I won't accept that. It sounds too like the subjective Idealism of Fichte. There must be objective truth somewhere; and all questions in religion and metaphysics run to this: where is objective truth to be found?

Now this little crossing of swords is all your fault. You achieve in your brief lines, what I have always been anxious to achieve in larger spaces, i.e., you provoke controversy. The best compliment that can be paid to an author is to challenge him; and I want to know what are "the ends outside ourselves."[13]

When he comes to write again, Wendell does not really answer the canon's question. He merely says that he defines truth as "the system of my limitations," but goes on happily to respond to Sheehan's warning: "When you say I have aroused the Celt in you, I grin with joy—though you don't give me a real whack on the head—but it reminds me of what Lady Alice Gaisford once wrote me, that a friendship wasn't cemented until you had quarrelled—although we are still a good way from having done so."[14]

In October 1912, Canon Sheehan wrote Wendell that he had been in the South Infirmary in Cork since June as the result of a collapse which was a stage in an illness which offered no hope of cure.[15] The effect upon Wendell was instantaneous and obvious. From this point on, his letters show constant interest, intense solicitude and deep affection.

He writes not only to inquire as to the canon's condition, but to divert his mind from his suffering by telling of people who admired his novels, retailing political gossip, discussing philosophers of mutual interest, reporting on his speeches, and describing books he had just read. He apologizes for the nature of some of his discussion, but explains: "I talk on, hoping to give you a moment's distraction, not that I am not thinking of you all the time." At the end of a later letter, he justifies its discursive nature: "Dear friend, again understand that I write about other things than yourself only because I hope I may amuse or distract you."[16]

Wendell was not one to slop over in his correspondence and in the fifty-eight years of his writing to Pollock, he addressed him as "Fred" only once. With Sheehan, however, his tone became much warmer after he learned of his friend's physical collapse. He addressed him as "My dear friend" while he signed himself, "Ever affectionately," "Always affectionately and sincerely," and "Ever yours affectionately." "Meantime be sure of my constant affection," he wrote and " . . .you give such comfort and joy to one at least who loves you." Several times, he writes that he is sending his "love."

His interest is constant and compelling. "I grieve to think that you have days of pain," he writes, and, in another place, "I think of you a great deal and am always hoping that you may not be suffering." Again: "Your letter gives me the heart ache. I have been thinking so much about and hoping so much for good news."

Wendell's affection was reciprocated by the canon. He subscribed his letters "Affectionately" and "Alway affectionately," and when he wrote Wendell from the Infirmary in 1912, he acknowledged: "Your friendship is one of the sheet-anchors of life." He signed it, "Ever affectionately, dear Dr. Holmes . . ."

The last letter in the correspondence was written by Canon Sheehan on June 21, 1913 and it expressed his delight on learning that Wendell, who was in London, was coming on to visit him in Doneraile.

The final line read: "Need I say what a ray of sunshine your visit will cast over a broken life like mine." His last words, "Always affectionately & sincerely" might well serve as a description of their entire exchange of letters.[17]

Wendell did in fact visit Doneraile and a letter to Pollock reveals that he saw Sheehan at that time and that "the Canon considered himself a dying man and though we had a cheerful daily talk, *that* was in the background." Before Wendell left, he and the canon went through a most appropriate ritual. "Before I left, he asked me to choose a book from his library, with the result that I sent a folio Suarez *De Legibus* home by post. He thought that Suarez[18] was the *ne plus ultra* of original philosophy, as to which I naturally remain a sceptic until converted."

Although neither could know it, Canon Sheehan was to die that same year. Here at his last opportunity, Wendell, by selecting the work of a Catholic philosopher, performed an act which he knew would please his old friend and one which symbolized to both the respect, constancy and affection of their remarkable relationship. With Wendell, this fascinating exchange of letters reveals a side of his character which is as ingratiating as it is unusual. It is an aspect of his personality which he was chary of showing since it embodied his substantial endowment of tenderness and affection. It marked a noteworthy departure from his lack of concern for problems of his fellow man.

Sheehan's analysis of Wendell is pertinent here: A tough-minded intellectual who was a "regular Danton-Herod[19] on paper and in theory," but was "not very hard hearted in practice."[20]

NOTES ON CANON FROM CORK

[1] David H. Burton, ed., *Holmes-Sheehan Correspondence* (New York: Kennikat Press, 1976), p. 6.

[2] Herman H. Heuser (1852–1933), American priest, founder of *American Ecclesiastical Review*, author of Sheehan's biography, *Canon Sheehan of Doneraile*.

[3] Holmes/Sheehan, Jan. 2, 1904, Burton, p. 12.

[4] Holmes/Sheehan, Feb. ——, 1904, Burton, p. 12.

[5] Sheehan/Holmes, Feb. 3, 1904, Burton, pp. 12, 13.

[6] Holmes/Sheehan, Mar. 21, 1908, Burton, p. 21.

[7] Holmes/Sheehan, Jul. 17, 1909, Burton, pp. 27, 28.

[8] Holmes/Sheehan, Aug. 14, 1910, Burton, p. 32.

[9] Robert Hugh Benson (1871–1914), English priest, writer and apologist. Holmes refers to "Catholicism and the Future," *The Atlantic Monthly,* CVI (1910), pp. 166–75.

[10] Sheehan/Holmes, Aug. 26, 1910, Burton, p. 33.

[11] Holmes/Sheehan, Mar. 1, 1911, Burton, p. 37.

[12] Holmes/Sheehan, Apr. 1, 1911, Burton, pp. 40, 41.

[13] Sheehan/Holmes, Aug. 4, 1911, Burton, pp. 42, 43.

[14] Holmes/Sheehan, Aug. 14, 1911, Burton, pp. 43, 44.

[15] Sheehan/Holmes, Oct. 16, 1912, Burton, p. 48.

[16] Holmes/Sheehan, Oct. 27, 1912, Burton, pp. 50, 51.

[17] Sheehan/Holmes, Jun. 21, 1913, Burton, p. 65.

[18] Francisco Suarez (1548–1617), Spanish Jesuit theologian, founder of the philosophy of international law. In *On Laws,* he attacked the divine right of kings and insisted that a just political order required the consent of the people.

[19] Georges Jacques Danton (1759–94), leader in the French Revolution, who had a role in the massacres attendant thereto.

Herod Antipas (?–40 A.D.), tetrarch of Galilee (4 B.C.–39 A.D.) who ordered the beheading of John the Baptist and participated in the trial of Jesus Christ.

[20] Burton, *Holmes-Sheehan Correspondence,* p. 6.

Some Can't Helps

MURDER OR IMPROVEMENT

Wendell loved to be read to and his regular sessions of oral reading became one of his greatest sources of pleasure. As we have seen, this custom began while he was still a judge on the Massachusetts Supreme Judicial Court; a doctor suggested that reading at night would be harmful to his eyes. At first, Fanny read to him in the evenings after dinner while he played solitaire. Their evenings were quiet because Wendell had consciously limited his socializing when he went on the court. He explained his policy to Owen Wister: "I don't somehow cotton to the idea of our Judges hobnobbing in hotel bars and saloons. The Bench should stand aloof from indiscriminate familiarities." Bit by bit, the reading custom became institutionalized, later was expanded to include his secretaries, and in his last days developed into an all-encompassing major portion of his life.

The formalization began when Wendell initiated the practice of recording the name, author and date of perusal of every book that was read to him. For this purpose, he used a hard-covered notebook—later known as the famous "Black Book"—wherein he had made entries, beginning in 1871, of the reading which he had done in the preparation of *The Common Law*. These notations were religiously made for over fifty years until the last was made in 1935 by his last secretary, James Rowe. That final book was a novel by Thornton Wilder.[1] Coming as it did just before Wendell's death, it was appropriately titled *Heaven Is My Destination*. Wendell's minuscule and often illegible handwriting crawls in columns down the pages and, finally, as the book becomes filled, is turned sideways and into the margins to use up each bit of white space. "He was too much of a Yankee," Tommy Corcoran observed, "to buy a new notebook."

The reading, in time, developed a number of accompanying conventions. Jim Rowe describes one:

103

He had a rule on reading. If you started a book, you had to finish it. We got into some real turkeys, you know, and I would say, "Mr. Justice, you don't like it, You can't stand it. You're not listening. I don't like it. Why don't we put it aside?" He would say, "No. If you start it, you have to finish it."

Wendell told Rowe: "I have to go in for some self-improvement every day" and Rowe comments: "That was the Yankee in him. You've got to go in for something that will improve you. And he did act according to this rule all his life. He was a very disciplined man."

One secretary's story illustrates the degree of Wendell's dedication to self-improvement:

When I was with him when he was eighty-eight, he began reading Thucydides in the original. He had never read Thucydides in the original. It is very difficult to read. I had studied Greek in college and realized that his Greek was still excellent. I asked him why he was burdening himself with this difficult reading at his stage of life and he said, "Well, when I appear before the *bon Dieu,* suppose he says, 'Holmes, can you recite on Thucydides?' and I have to say, 'Sire, I've never read him,' what a fool I'd feel."

Why he did it, I don't know. He did believe in what he called "improving the mind." On the other hand, he would sometimes read trivia such as Milt Gross's[2] Yiddish dialect stories of Bronx Jewish apartment house life. He read all sorts of mysteries and he particularly liked the Jeeves stories of P. G. Wodehouse.[3]

Chapman Rose, who was Wendell's secretary in 1931 and 1932, testifies, however, that this rule was not applied without exception.

The Justice had expressed an interest in D. H. Lawrence, having read reviews in the *Saturday Review.* . . . We ran out of the current book one night and he wanted to know what else we had and I told him that I had not read this, but it was *Lady Chatterly's Lover* and he said "Well, let's have a go at that." We got as far as page 107 and I was coughing and sputtering a little in reading this aloud to him. At this point, he roused up and said, "Sonny, we will not finish this book. It's dullness is not redeemed by its pornography." And there in his handwriting in the reading list is the confession of the sin of not finishing: "*Lady Chatterly's Lover,* Page 107—Whole book, Page 379."

The volume and variety of this reading stretches the understanding of the mind. Every form of literature was canvassed from classic epic to modern novel. Montesquieu, Thornton Wilder, Rabelais, Hemingway, Dante, Pierre Louÿs[4]—all were grist to the insatiable mill. Harold Laski, Felix Frankfurter, Justice Brandeis, Chief Justice Stone, Wendell's former secretaries—all conspired and cooperated to find books that would please him and satisfy his ravening appetite.

With his decreasing mobility, the reading became less a recreation and more a way of life and an obsession. From the simple reading of Fanny, this activity assumed such prominence in his life that relays of people were required to fill his available time. Not only did the current secretary read morning, afternoon, and evening, but former secretaries were pressed into service to fill in the gaps and even Mary Donnellan, the domestic chief of staff, was occasionally recruited for a spell of duty.

Tommy Corcoran, a secretary and later a volunteer companion recently talked of these sessions:

> By the time I was with them, the Holmeses were spending their evenings very quietly. They'd have supper and, afterward, she'd read to him a varied fare including all the naughty things she thought he'd like among the French novels. Later, the secretaries read to him, and the complete written list of his reading—his "Family Bible"—contains a listing of 3475 books. You'd have to read a book a day for ten years to equal this. Better than a book a week for the fifty odd years of his entries.
>
> If you look on the list, you'll find Bracton,[5] Descartes, the *Princesse de Clèves* of Madame de la Fayette—both the justice and Mrs. Holmes could read French—Adam Smith, *A Beautiful Scourge* by Gaboriau,[6] the French detective story writer, Balzac, Keats, *Burke's Appeal from the New to the Old Whigs,* Voltaire, Gertrude Atherton,[7] E. Phillips Oppenheim[8] and John Masefield.[9]
>
> Someone asked him why he read so much, even in his latter years. He said that he was reading for his last examination.

Corcoran extended the ambience of his readings when he came back to Washington in 1932, three years after Fanny's death:

> By this time, Holmes was no longer on the bench and I used to find him playing solitaire—which was symbolic to me. Since he

was not at court, his demands on his secretaries became that much greater and he used to wear them out reading to him. So I used to go over to I Street and read to him at night. I'd allocate my time so that I'd sleep in the afternoon and then come to him before going to work at night.

He'd sit in a chair which was upholstered in black leather and I would start to read and he would start to think. Then, he'd start to talk. He talked about everything under the sun. I read perhaps a hundred pages a night. He talked about the democratic process and the prospects for its survival and how strong his feeling was that this was *his* country. His grandmother had seen the British march into Boston and he, himself, had fought in the Civil War.

At that time, I was living in a little attic room on N Street. I have never lived on less in terms of social life, but I have never lived higher intellectually than I did then.

Wendell was punctilious in the standard he required of his readers. He was almost fanatical in his rubrics of pronunciation. Donald Hiss has said:

> When you mispronounced a word, he'd say, "Don't be an idiot, boy." He was extremely careful on pronunciation, for example, he would say "et" where I would say "ate." He had definite ideas of how the English language should be pronounced. One word I had difficulty in reading to him was *éxquisite*. I read *exquísite* and he corrected me and glared at me. I said, "Mr. Justice, I'm sorry, but I had a cousin in Baltimore who was very affected and she used to pronounce the word *exquísite* and I think this has just put a blockage up which I can't get over." He said, "Oh, you did son. Well, I had a cousin who once pronounced it *exquísite* and I thought I should have slapped her to the ground."

Even Mary Donnellan, the domestic major domo, who at times was pressed into service if a secretary was absent, was not permitted to proceed without control. "Sometimes," Mary has said, "if the secretary went downtown and wasn't coming back, I'd do a bit of reading and if I made a mistake, he'd always correct me. 'Mary, No!' he'd say. And then he'd tell me what the word was."

His choice of a book always involved a certain amount of cogitation. "Well, Sonny," he would say to his secretary, "what shall it be, murder or improvement?" and, to rationalize a selection of the former, he might say half-apologetically, "Well, ninety-one outlives duty, let's read E. Phillips Oppenheim," referring to an English author, then popular, whose novels of adventure and intrigue were great favorites of his.

Mark Howe has provided further evidence of Wendell's taste in novel structure: "We finished Kenneth Roberts's[10] *Rabble in Arms* to-day which I rather insisted on his liking—but he really did, I think. Just before the end, I asked him whether he wanted it to have a happy or a tragic ending. He said, 'Oh, a happy one—I like happy endings.'"

Later Howe made the following entry in his diary: "Reading Alice Longworth's *Crowded Hours* which he doesn't like. He finds one of the nicest things about T.R. is his relation with his family—his interest in all their activities. He said about the book that he doesn't see how it can be considered a legitimate subject of interest to anyone."

The newspaper was an exception to his wide-ranging ingestion of printed matter. He simply didn't read the daily newspaper. "If anything important happens," he said, "my friends will tell me about it." Donald Hiss has noted: "He never read any newspaper. He would read magazines—he looked at the *New Republic*. I think that went back to Herbert Croly's[11] day. He read *The Atlantic Monthly*. He would call them 'silly things' if he saw me reading a newspaper. He would say, 'Do you read them?' and I would say, 'Yes. Every day' and he would say, 'They are superficial, silly things.'"

Jim Rowe tells of Wendell's rejection of a book when he was in his ninety-fourth year:

Somebody sent him a book on the immortality of the soul. I think it was a collection of pieces by Plato and Aristotle and everybody who had ever talked about the immortality of the soul. I said to him, "Mr. Justice, would you like to read this?" It was a gift. "No," he said. "Well," I said to myself, "here I am at 25 and here's this old fellow at 93. He ought to be thinking about this." So, I said, "Aren't you interested in the immortality of the soul?" "No," he said. "I used to be when I was young, but now the subject bores me. Let's read that detective story."

As Rowe points out, Wendell, was not uniformly enthusiastic about books sent to him by his friends: "He'd say, for instance,

'Oh my God, Brandeis has sent me another book. I'll hurt his feeling if I don't read it, but I hate it. It's so dull.' "

Originally a source of relaxation, Wendell's oral reading became for him a powerful drug that he could not do without. It provided stimulation for his mind and, at the same time, insulated him from the confusion and moils of everyday life. Certainly, there have been few nonprofessional practitioners of letters in history who have had the inclination and opportunity to make the absorption of literature such a major part of their lives and who have shown such sensitive appreciation of the printed word in all its forms. Even if he lived today in an age of radio, television and movies, one suspects that Wendell's interest would remain very much as it was in his time.

OTHER RECREATIONS

For one whose youth had been so full of violent activity—and perhaps because of it—Wendell's methods of relaxation were largely sedentary. His reading, as we have seen, even involved the active participation of a lector, not of himself. He had to take lessons to learn how to ride a bicycle at the age of fifty-four. Learning this new skill was so exciting to him that he had to write to Lady Pollock about his performance several times. This seems to have been his most vigorous exercise.

Besides reading, his aesthetic interests were directed toward prints and engravings in which he maintained a passionate and lifelong absorption. He not only read about prints and collected them himself, but he studied the methods of print-making.

He developed a close friendship with Richard Austin Rice, the head of the print department at the Library of Congress, and nothing would please Wendell more than to stroll from the Supreme Court for a session of examining the Library print collection with Rice. He was familiar with the Rembrandts and the Meryons (one stood on the mantel in his study), but he also knew the Elsheimers[12] and the Uffenbachs.[13] He owned a Nanteuil[14] engraving and several Van Dyck[15] etchings as well as a Dürer[16] woodcut. He was expert enough to be able to go over prints with a glass to determine their stages in the printing process. His collection included not only the masters, but an occasional light and even salacious subject. He had some skill as an artist himself and one of his early sketches is reproduced in the first volume of Howe's biography. He bequeathed his collection to the Library of Congress and his prints and lithographs may now be examined at the library building in Washington.

Another recreation was the Holmes's regular Friday night visit to the theatre. He and Fanny started this regular jaunt when they lived in Boston and they continued it as long as she was able to accompany him. After she ceased to attend the theatre, as we have seen, Wendell enjoyed regular visits to the Gayety burlesque.

Wendell seems to have had a blind (perhaps one should say "deaf") spot where music was concerned. One finds almost no reference to music in his letters. The few in the Pollock group which refer to music simply mention Spengler's[17] placing of *Parsifal* as the peak of modern artistic achievement, but contain no comment to indicate agreement, disagreement, or even understanding. One looks in vain for references to folk songs (he must have heard his father-in-law sing), group singing, marching songs in the war, band concerts, operas or symphonic presentations. There is one story of his hesitant attendance at a recital by the great Russian basso, Feodor Chaliapin, where the seats cost five dollars, then a considerable sum, and his return to tell his secretary that the experience was not worth the cost. Apparently, he did not thrill to the famous rendition of "The Volga Boat Song."[18]

Perhaps the only record of Wendell's attention to music of any sort was his encouragement of Timmy O'Brien, a friend in Beverly Farms who played the accordion and sang Irish songs. Wendell had him come up to the Holmes house to perform on his squeeze box and combine his ballads with Irish reels.[19] With typical hyperbole, Wendell told O'Brien that he would rather hear him sing "My Wild Irish Rose" than listen to grand opera. Or perhaps it was not hyperbole.

It was in the realm of the mind that Wendell found his real recreation. His speculation and mental exploration began early in Cambridge with his friend William James and another friend John Chipman Gray. He was most at ease in small groups, especially of young people, although he enjoyed making a formal speech at a grand occasion, such as a Brown Commencement or a meeting of the Boston Bar. His insatiable curiosity and love of philosophical gymnastics continued throughout his life. But, in a sense, all his knowledge and his command of centuries of philosophical commentary had left him in no haven of certitude. The editor of the Holmes-Einstein letters, James Bishop Peabody,[20] called him "a skeptic but no cynic and an agnostic but no atheist."

For him, fun was "firing off" a letter to Pollock or Laski or Einstein or Lady Cas .etown or Baroness Moncheur with a new and arresting epigram; it was writing a thundering opinion from which "the genitalia" would not be cut off by his colleagues on the bench. In his youth, his heart had been "touched with fire," as he had said, and he had certainly earned the right to a life that would embrace a reasonable amount of thought and philosophizing. Of course, his duties as a judge entailed constant hard and demanding work and a certain amount of social activity. But he always longed to retire to his study where his real life was lived. One may regret the degree of his withdrawal from contact with his fellowman and his concerns. He accused his friend, Henry Adams, of "posing to himself as the old cardinal where he would turn everything to dust and ashes"[21] in the solitude of his house on H Street. But perhaps Wendell was more like Adams than he would have liked to admit. At any rate, such was his personality.

NOTES ON SOME CAN'T HELPS

[1] Thornton Niven Wilder (1897–1975), teacher and internationally noted American novelist and playwright. Author of *Our Town, The Bridge of San Luis Rey* and *The Matchmaker* from which last *Hello Dolly,* the musical, was adapted.

[2] Milt Gross (1895–1953), American cartoonist in New York papers, author of highly popular Jewish dialect books—*Nize Baby; Dunt Esk; Hiawatta With No Odder Poems.*

[3] P. (Pelham) G. (Grenville) (Plum) Wodehouse (1881–1975), noted English-born humorist who not only created Jeeves and Bertie Wooster, but also wrote the lyrics for "Bill" which Helen Morgan sang in Jerome Kern's *Show Boat.* Became an American citizen in 1955.

[4] Pierre Louÿs (1870–1925), French man of letters, author of works of daring sensuality such as *Aphrodite,* written in a refined and supple style.

[5] Marie Madeleine, Comtesse de La Fayette (1634–1693), *précieuse,* French novelist and author of letters and interesting *Mémoires.*

[6] Émile Gaboriau (1885–1973), popular French author of detective stories such as *La Corde Au Cou,* creator of M. Le Coq, famous fictional detective.

[7] Gertrude Atherton (1857–1948), California-born American novelist, author of *The Californians, The Horn of Life*, etc.

[8] E(dward). Phillips Oppenheim (1866–1946), prolific and highly popular British author of whodunits, producing as many as three annually of thrillers such as *Clowns and Criminals* and *Shudders and Thrills*.

[9] John Masefield (1878–1967), British poet, Poet Laureate from 1930, author of *Salt Water Poems and Ballads, The Widow in the Bye Street* and *The Nine Days Wonder* (on the Dunkirk evacuation in W.W. II).

[10] Kenneth (Lewis) Roberts (1885–1957), newspaperman and popular American writer of historical novels such as *Rabble in Arms, Northwest Passage* and *Oliver Wiswell*.

[11] Herbert Croly (1869–1930), author, political philosopher and editor who supported a strong central government and large labor unions, was a founder of the *New Republic* magazine and a friend of Frankfurter and Laski whose writings often appeared in the columns of his magazine.

[12] Adam Elsheimer (1578–1620), Dutch printmaker, follower of Uffenbach.

[13] Philipp Uffenbach (1570–1630), Dutch printmaker and precursor of Rembrandt.

[14] Robert Nanteuil (1623–1678), French engraver whose portraits included all the best-known figures of his time.

[15] Anthony Van Dyck (1599–1641), Belgian-born painter and printmaker. One of the greatest artists of the Flemish school.

[16] Albrecht Dürer (1471–1528), celebrated German engraver, painter, sculptor and architect. His works are invaluable historical documents.

[17] Oswald Spengler (1880–1936), gloomy German philosopher, author of *Der Untergang des Abendlands*, current in the 1920s, in which he held that the West was in a period of decay.

[18] Feodor Chaliapin (1873–1938), famous Russian basso, noted for his womanizing, his roles of Boris Godunov and Mephistopheles in addition to his rendition of the *Volga Boat Song*.

[19] Wendell once told Barton Leach that he "hated music."

[20] James Bishop Peabody, Harvard LL.B 1950; d. March 22, 1977.

[21] Howe, *Holmes–Pollock Letters*, vol. 2, p. 18.

Wendell's Boys

In 1905, the third year after taking his seat on the Supreme Court of the United States, Wendell began the custom of designating a young law school graduate to be his secretary for one year; he continued this practice until his death thirty years later. The roster of these secretaries contains the names of men who later became famous for their achievements in law, politics, public life and industry.

His first appointee, was Charles K. Poe, a graduate of George Washington College and Law School in Washington, D.C., the only one on the list who was not a graduate of the Harvard Law School. The favored thirty included: Augustin Derby, professor of law at the New York University School of Law and later dean of the law school of the University of Virginia; Irving S. Olds, chairman of the United States Steel Corporation; Francis Biddle, attorney general of the United States; George L. Harrison, president of the New York Life Insurance Company, Laurence Curtis, member of Congress from Massachusetts; W. Barton Leach, professor of law at the Harvard Law School; Thomas G. Corcoran, New Deal legislative craftsman and intimate advisor of President Franklin D. Roosevelt; Alger Hiss, organizer of the Dumbarton Oaks conference on the formation of the United Nations and principal in the perjury *cause célèbre* of the early 1950s; H. Chapman Rose, under secretary of the U.S. Treasury; Mark De Wolfe Howe, Jr., professor of law at the Harvard Law School and biographer of Wendell; and James H. Rowe, administrative assistant to President Franklin D. Roosevelt, member of the Hoover Commission and chairman of the Twentieth Century Fund.

Wendell based his early invitations to serve upon the recommendations of John Chipman Gray, a Boston contemporary and professor at the Harvard Law School. When Gray died, Dean Ezra Ripley Thayer, also of Harvard, was consulted, and in the latter years, Professor Felix Frankfurter was the authorized nominator. The nominees were picked from the top scholastic levels of the third year class and were generally, but not always, of Law Review rank. Temperamental harmony with Wendell was an ever-present consideration, of course.

Unlike the "law clerks" of today the duties of Wendell's nominees *were* largely secretarial. Their main law-connected obligation was to review for him the petitions for *certiorari*, the "petes for cert" or "bloody certs," as he called them, which were applications to bring to the Court cases which otherwise had no absolute right to a hearing. Many were filed, but few were granted, and the business of considering and making a determination on each was a demanding and petty obligation. Wendell asked his secretary to read and report on each one. Then Wendell would make a decision on his recommendation for action in the later conference by the full complement of justices. Beyond this, the secretary did not enter into the judging process. Wendell knew the cases he wanted to cite, many were decisions by his "favorite author," i.e. himself, and he wrote his opinions in longhand, standing at his grandfather's desk, immediately upon assignment by the chief justice.

The secretary, however, was expected to engage in a variety of nonlegal activities. These included paying the household and personal bills, keeping the checkbooks in balance, going on Wendell's daily walks while he was still active and taking automobile rides when his physical debility had made walking impossible. The young man appeared as a factotum at the Monday receptions while Fanny was alive and active and wrote the ministerial letters which Wendell's position required. The substantial letters he reserved for himself, writing each one in longhand without keeping a copy of any kind.

Only on the rarest of occasions would he consider delegating the writing of one of the letters in the latter category. "I made the mistake once," said Donald Hiss, "in suggesting that I might write a reply to a letter which Pollock had written to him. I did this because he was not feeling well that day. He said, 'No, no, I'll do it.' Then he said, 'Maybe you could at that.' Then I was caught and I asked, 'What will I say?' He laughed and said, 'Oh, just stir up the mud a bit.' Then I got cold feet and backed off. I said, 'I guess you had better do it yourself, Mr. Justice.'"

The duties of Wendell's secretaries were modest in comparison, for example, with those of Mr. Justice Brandeis, who labored night and day to compile the mass of facts and authorities which he required for his opinions. In fact, Barton Leach has stated that while the court was sitting, he found time for more golf while he was with Wendell than he had been able to play for a long time.

Wendell had a warm feeling for his "boys" as he called his secretaries. "There was a human warmth that one felt about him," Chapman Rose has said, "but not to the extent that he considered us 'sons by adoption' or 'substitute sons' as was suggested by Emmet Lavery in his play, 'The Magnificent Yankee.'" He was intensely interested in the thoughts and feelings of these young men and there is no doubt that contact with them maintained the freshness of his outlook. He had his favorites, of course, including George Harrison, Tommy Corcoran, and Laury Curtis. "He opened himself more fully to these," said Barton Leach, "than he did to some of the others." Leach felt that he was not one of the favorites and there was in his assessment the implication that, to some extent, the warmth of Wendell's attachment was affected by the degree to which the secretary flattered him and submitted to his influence. However, Rose never found the affection equated with adulation and, in any event, the difference in feeling was relative and the bonds forged during each secretaryship remained strong for the remainder of Wendell's life.

Wendell was once asked why he went to the trouble of bringing on and breaking in a new secretary every year. He answered that he liked to continue to tell his fund of stories; this way, he could do so without being accused of repeating himself.

The Holmes graduates formed a *de facto* alumni association of impressive power and ability, but there never was any concerted action as a unit. Ranging from dedicated New Dealer to conservative Legionnaire, their points of view were too diverse for any such collaboration, even if it had been considered. Their joint activities were limited to an occasional social meeting such as that held at the Harvard Law School on the fortieth anniversary of Wendell's death; the old boys gathered, retold the famous stories, and relived the exciting days of their youth.

I've previously referred to another celebrated gathering of the alumni, conceived by Fanny and held on Wendell's eightieth birthday, March 8, 1921. The former secretaries were bidden from all over to Washington. They secretly arrived at I Street and gathered behind closed doors in the dining room. Wendell had anticipated dinner at a restaurant. When he came downstairs from dressing, the dining room doors were flung open and he was greeted by his boys, all in full dinner dress. Uncharacteristically, he failed to find words to express his astonishment.

For the secretaries, the year with Wendell was as educational as their course at Harvard. They heard his stories about the Civil War, his comments on judges and lawyers and his analyses of the events of the day. In addition, he occasionally sought to test their minds and deepen their understanding of philosophy or ethics, history or religion. He maintained that he engaged his secretaries for only one year because in that time he could give all he had to give, but this was manifestly not so since some secretaries who returned on a voluntary basis after their regular stint found his speculations and insights as fascinating as ever.

His method of exposition might be to pop a philosophical question at an unsuspecting young man—as he did one day with Donald Hiss: "Sonny, if you were at war and had your rifle raised and brought into your sights an enemy figure and God tapped you on the shoulder and said, 'If you let that man live, he'll be a great doctor some day,' what would you do?" Hiss replied that the question required thought and and that he couldn't give a ready answer. "Don't be an idiot, boy," came the prompt response. "He's the enemy and you'd shoot him of course. You're not God, you are merely a soldier fighting a war."

His speculations were often expressed spontaneously. One secretary recalled an example of this type of query. He and Wendell had been on one of their recreational automobile rides, as often, to the grounds of the Franciscan Monastery in far Northeast Washington. The grounds of the monastery have always been beautifully kept and the order had a particularly fine rose garden which Wendell loved. "Why can't these people," he asked, referring to the religious society, "who appreciate all this beauty be more open-minded? Can you understand, Sonny, how they can be so rigid?"

In other instances, Wendell's method of educating his young men was more extended and intensive. Such was with Tommy

TOMMY-THE-CORK IN FULL FLIGHT. Thomas G. Corcoran, secretary and intimate of Wendell, discusses his days with the justice (1979).

WENDELL'S CHIEF OF STAFF. Annie M. (Donnellan) Coakley, manager of the household, confidante and friend recalls experiences at 1720 I Street (1979).

Corcoran who received a course on the Bible. "I suppose
you've read the New Testament," Wendell said to Corcoran
one day. The latter answered "Of course." "Of course, as a
Catholic, you had to," Wendell continued, "but did you ever
read the Old Testament?" Tommy answered, "Not so much."
Corcoran added, "Then the justice said, 'You know, I walk
every afternoon for exercise and I take my secretary along. I
like to talk and I'd like to know what you're thinking about.
Suppose we begin to talk about fundamentals. Get a copy of the
Old Testament. Don't get one of those old things like the
Gideon Bible where all the books are lying together like her-
rings in a box. There's a new edition of the Bible called *The
Modern Reader's Bible* and it separates the various biblical
elements. I want you to read three or four chapters of this
Modern Reader's Bible. You won't find it hard work.' "

"This publication," Corcoran went on, "was the first attempt to separate, in the spirit of the Bible, what was poetry,
like the Song of Solomon, what was drama, like Job, and what
the Justice called 'the footnotes,' which were the 'begats and
begats' and were really the ancestral records of the people."
Corcoran continued:

> So, I began this reading and he'd talk about it as showing the
> sociological evolution of the Jewish people and, beyond that,
> he'd discuss the question of whether, in terms of divine revela-
> tion, the fundamental precepts of a religion were any more than
> the enlightenment of some statesman who put in the guise of
> "God's religion"—because everything was then put in the guise
> of "God's religion"—the fundamental rules by which a society
> had to live if it were going to be stable.
>
> He started with the Ten Commandments. "There may be a
> question," he said, "whether or not Moses actually brought
> down from the mountain top those tablets of stone with their
> inscription of the Ten Commandments, nevertheless, these were
> the perceptions of a great political organizer who understood
> that he was dealing with the problem of holding his little band
> together and, whether it was divine revelation or not, it was very
> interesting that they somehow coincided.
>
> "For instance, take 'I am the Lord thy God. Thou shalt not
> have other gods before me.' This is what *we* call the F.B.I.
> statute. It says that you can't go chasing around with foreign
> enemies." Then we went through some of the other command-

ments. "What do men fight about? Men fight about property.
'Thou shalt not covet thy neighbor's goods.' They fight about
women. 'Thou shalt not covet thy neighbor's wife.' They fight
over being lied about in a court of justice. 'Neither shalt thou
bear false witness against thy neighbor.'

"Then," he said, "there's that interesting one, the fifth. Now,
Son, recite on that commandment." So, I went merrily along
and I said, "Honor thy father and thy mother."

"Come on, Son," he said, "the most important part is what
goes after that." I said, "I know there's some kind of con-
secutive clause to the effect that thy days may be prolonged and
that it may go well with thee, and he said, "Yes. Do you understand what that means?" I said, "No. Not quite." He said,
"Son, that represents the point where the wandering Hebrew
ceased to be a nomadic people and became an agricultural
people. In a nomadic civilization, the old lady and the old man
are left behind to starve or they're knocked on the head whenever they're no longer able to perform their economic services
for a people who are really up against it for the necessities of
life. But when they become a settled or agricultural people, a
wise old geezer like me goes to a young chump like you and
says, 'These nights, your mother and I get nervous because we
wonder if one of these days we're going to be knocked on the
head.' Then the old man explains to his son that the reason for
doing away with the old folks goes back to the conditions of a
long time ago. 'Look around now,' the father says. 'There's corn
in the crib. There's sheep in the fold. There's plenty to eat. You
don't need to continue the old custom. You can spare your
mother and me and, if you do, *thy* days will be prolonged in the
land which the Lord, thy God, giveth thee.' "

Holmes had me read all his opinions from the beginning of
his time on the Massachusetts court to his latest on the Supreme
Court. He had me read *The Education of Henry Adams* and the
historical critiques of Henry's brother, Brooks, who was a Bryan
Democrat and a very enlightened guy. The objective here was
for me to understand the modern philosopher. He used to say
that one ought to know about ancient philosophy, but that every
later commentator had added something to the ancient and that
the older works should be read only with the moderns in mind.

He was constantly interested in the relation of man to the
universe and, at the same time, he was as concrete as he could
be. He used to say, "Every generalization is worthless, including this one." He also said, "You can dream and you can dream
and you can dream, but when you come back to everyday

affairs, it's a salutary thing to have commanded men under fire when, by God, if you made a mistake, somebody died."

One summer, I was invited to go down to the Holmes summer home in Beverly Farms. He and Mrs. Holmes liked me because I added some life to the dull routine on the North Shore. I was also invited because of my willingness to argue with him—and I argued a great deal. And I learned a lot from him. I'm a much different Catholic from having been with him. I think he saw the true function of the church in society more clearly than most of the priests and bishops.

He used to quote Goethe's aphorism that "On the mountain-top, all paths unite." If you were big enough, you saw the whole thing. Through this approach, he made me very understanding about the mutations while realizing that the fundamental principles stay the same.

He would say that there was no such thing as an objective standard of justice because you have an idea of justice and I have an idea of justice. It is a very subjective thing. But the function of law is to make objective some kind of compromise so that while everyone would not agree, and some might disagree as much as 20 percent, people would go along and obey. This was the cost they paid for stability in everything they cared about, whether it was their personal property, their land or their family.

It was through this method of education that Holmes unified my attitude towards the whole social and economic system as nobody else could have.

He had an example to illustrate his interest in specifics. "When you're up against a particular proposition," he said, "you must remember *Uncle Tom's Cabin,* where Eliza in mid-winter was crossing the Ohio on the ice. Her problem all the time was with the next piece of ice."

Corcoran concluded with a moving appraisal: "Being with this man was an incredible personal experience and his ideas were burned into me so deeply that I have made evaluations by his standards ever since. It was an extraordinary exercise in thinking as high up as you could and, at the same time, never forgetting the next piece of ice."

Wendell had in theory a rule that his secretaries not be married; he wished to have a young man available as an extra man or as a substitute at parties and receptions. An additional reason, and perhaps the controlling one, was that one of the secretaries had got married before he began his service and, in the words of Katharine Bundy, "was a mess because he was moony and lovesick." At least two secretaries, Leach and Alger Hiss, married in ignorance or defiance of the regulation, but Wendell became adjusted to the situation in each case. Leach explained his method of conciliation: "It really irked him that I had been so inconsiderate as to get myself married. However, when my wife and I first dined with the Holmeses, I made it clear that it was her job to reconcile him to the situation. She did."

In the case of the Bundys, as we have already noted, Wendell gave his approval to their marriage in the middle of Harvey's term, impelled by Fanny's industrious missionary work.

Every secretary considered it a rare privilege to share in the life of one of the authentically great men of the history of the United States. They enjoyed the talk on all subjects, the fun, the banter. They cherished the opportunity to see him at work, to take care of his business needs, to assist, to a small degree, in the processing of his court work. They relished the surroundings in which they worked: the two great studies, back to back, with their crammed bookcases, the mantel with the Meryon etchings, the crossed swords over the fireplace, the light streaming in the two rear windows; Wendell would stand at his writing desk or less frequently sit at the great desk which had belonged to the Autocrat of the Breakfast Table and smoke a fragrant Havana cigar. "Well, now, Sonny," he might say, "what do you think of that opinion that I gave you to read?"

"I think, Sir, that the opinion is splendid, except for the last paragraph which seems to me to be not quite clear."

"What the hell do you mean—not quite clear? Give it to me." He would read it. "Well, if you don't understand it, I suppose there'll be some other damn fool who won't. So I'd better change it."

These were memories to be treasured.

For many of the secretaries, there was also the delight of knowing Fanny Holmes.

Wendell followed the careers of his alumni with deep interest and answered their communications with scrupulous regularity. Following are two examples from letters received by Laurence Curtis:

Supreme Court of the United States
Washington, D.C.

Nov. 18, 1926

My dear Curtis

It was not until I had spent every spare minute in browsing
over the Dictionary of Modern English Usage for forty eight
hours that just now I discovered your card. You couldn't have
given me more pleasure unless by turning up yourself. The book
is so good and so corroborates my prejudices, even at times
unexpectedly, as in the pronunciation of girls, that I whinny
with delight. Hitherto I have regarded a catalogue of second
hand books as the best reading but now I dont know but I must
give this first place. I thank you most sincerely and heartily.

Ever sincerely yours
OWHolmes

The second was written six months after Fanny's death and
reflects the sadness of life without her:

Supreme Court of the United States
Washington, D.C.

Oct 25 1929

My dear Curtis

Good luck to you in the election and thanks for the book to
come.

Of course come to Washington I shall hope to see you. Food
is to be had at 1720 I Street, N.W. at 1 *30* if the Court is not
sittng. Or almost always at 7 p.m. but a solitary old man would
be your only companion. He is visible at other times after 11 Am
or 5 p.m. barring occasional engagement.

Sincerely
OW.Holmes

Wendell kept a watchful, and sometimes amused, eye upon
his boys. Augustin Derby cites an instance in his memoir in the
New York Law Quarterly Review:

Soon after my arrival in Washington, I came down with a touch of malaria, and was advised by my physician to rest in bed for a short while. This must have been a disappointment to the Justice, for afterwards I learned that he had been troubled in previous years by absences of his staff, on pleasure bent; which explains his greeting on my return to duty. With a twinkle in his eye he said, "Well, Derby, I should have come round to see you, but I thought you might have been having a bit of a time."

Derby's appraisal of Wendell might well serve as the expression of the sentiments of all the secretaries: "It was not for his learning that his secretaries revered him or as the 'great liberal,' or the 'great dissenter.' It was for the greatness of his personal qualities, his humanity and understanding, his rare charm, and warm friendship."

The place which this succession of young men held in Wendell's heart may be inferred from an exchange quoted by Derby: ". . . long after my day, one of them [the secretaries] had the courage, or audacity, to ask him whether it had not been a great regret to him that he had had no children. His answer in effect was, 'Why should it be. I have had all of you young men year after year.'"

The place Wendell held in the hearts of his secretaries is succinctly expressed in the conclusion of Barton Leach: "But let there be no doubt about this: Whatever cliché may have been uttered about great men and their valets, Holmes, J. is a hero to his secretaries."

Politics

While in Massachusetts, Wendell voted as a Republican, and he remained one in sympathy after he moved to the District of Columbia where the residents could not vote in presidential elections. As a young man in Boston with its antislavery and pro-Union sentiments, it was natural for him to support the party of Lincoln and Senator Charles Sumner.[1] In later years despite a variety of candidates and a diversity of political conditions, his feelings always remained the same. It was natural enough for him to back Theodore Roosevelt even though Wendell had reservations about T.R's intellectual capacity and scrupulousness. On the other hand, Wendell's obligations were not the same with Coolidge in 1924 and Hoover in 1928 and 1932, but he told Harold Laski that he would have cast his ballot for them against Smith and F.D. Roosevelt respectively if it had been legally possible for him to vote. He even defended Coolidge against Laski's criticism. It is worth noting that Holmes never seemed to feel urgently enough about voting to register in Beverly Farms Massachusetts. As he owned the house there until his death he might have made this his voting residence without undue scruple.

In an important sense, Wendell owed his judicial career to the Republican Party; a Republican governor had appointed him to the Supreme Judicial Court of Massachusetts, another had appointed him chief justice, and a Republican president had nominated him to the Supreme Court of the United States; Republican members of the concerned legislative bodies had confirmed his designation. For these reasons alone, loyalty might have dictated his allegiance. In addition, that loyalty might have been deepened by the course taken by the process of his elevation to the nation's highest tribunal.

The process of making Wendell a justice and later chief justice in his home state proceeded without event or complication. In fact, when the latter position became vacant it was considered to be properly his. With the federal post, however, the course was much more complicated, as Professor John A. Garraty[2] demonstrated in his article on Wendell's appointment in the September 1949 *New England Quarterly.*[3]

To begin with, there was business opposition to Wendell because of his liberal views on labor and the right of workers to organize. This opposition developed support for other candidates, including the nephew of George Frisbie Hoar,[4] the senior senator from Massachusetts. This, in and of itself, did not concern Theodore Roosevelt who would make the nomination and wanted a reasonably liberal justice, but he was troubled by the lack of acquiescence from Senator Hoar who, among other reasons for recalcitrance, was miffed because the president seemed to be rushing into the nomination without consulting him. Henry Cabot Lodge, the junior senator from Massachusetts and Wendell's prime supporter, sought to placate Hoar, but this was not easy. "I have never heard anybody speak of Judge Holmes as an able judge," the unhappy senior senator told Lodge. "He is universally regarded as a man of pleasant personal address . . . but without strength, and without grasp of general principles." Apparently, Hoar had not read *The Common Law.* He felt, he asserted, like a Worcester lawyer who heard that a neighbor was going to shoot his dog, "If he gives me notice and then shoots my dog, I don't care, but if he shoots my dog without giving me notice, I shall be mad."

Lodge and Wendell were also faced with an additional and equally delicate problem. This was to satisfy the simplistic president that Wendell would be "sound" on several forthcoming major politico-legal issues which would be coming before the Supreme Court. Roosevelt was concerned that the White House not be hampered in its freedom to deal as it wished with Puerto Rico and other territories. The Court had been precariously balanced on this point. Lodge consulted Wendell and then informed the president that he would not be "adverse" on "Porto [*sic*] Rican cases." Roosevelt, citing a recent speech of Wendell about Chief Justice Marshall, indicated his belief that a good judge should also be a good party man. He asked assurance on this point also and authorized Lodge to put the question to the candidate. The senator immediately conferred with Wendell.

"I told the President that you had always been a Republican

and never a Mugwump," said Lodge. And Lodge reported
Wendell's reply to the president: "A Mugwump! I should think
not. Why they are mere elements of dissolution."

Garraty asserts that Lodge could have had no doubt of
Wendell's regularity and cites authority to show that in 1884,
Wendell was "one of the few who stood up for him and sup-
ported him cordially" when most of Boston was scornful of
Lodge and his friends were cutting him on the street for sup-
porting James G. Blaine,[5] "the continental liar from the State of
Maine," for president.

Even after these assurances, Wendell was required to go to
Oyster Bay to talk with Roosevelt in person to satisfy the
president's requirements for the laying on of hands.

Although Hoar continued to growl that Wendell's "accom-
plishments are literary and social . . . not judicial . . . In his
opinions he runs to subtleties and refinements; and no decision
of his makes a great landmark in jurisprudence," he recognized
that there was personal political danger in opposing the nomination; he eventually became "reconciled if not satisfied."
Roosevelt thereupon proceeded to announce the nomination on
August 11, 1902, and it was consented to by the Senate on
December fourth and the new justice was sworn in on December eighth.

As Garraty wrote, "The amazing thing about the entire
episode of Holmes's appointment to the Supreme Court was
that neither the press nor the figures who played any important
part in it appreciated what was happening." Not only was
Wendell's true scholarly status disregarded, but his legal philosophy of legislative freedom for experimental social action
was ignored. His respect for the achievements of industrial
magnates who built colossal enterprises was not considered
either and this lack of comprehension was to cause bitterness
between the president and Wendell when the latter voted
against the majority in the *Northern Securities Company* case
in which the administration was trying to dissolve a combination of railroad companies.

Roosevelt, who was not a lawyer, later complained to Lodge:
"Nothing has been so strongly borne in on me concerning
lawyers on the bench as that the *nominal* politics of the man
has nothing to do with his actions on the bench. His *real*

politics are all important. From his antecedents, Holmes should have been an ideal man on the bench. As a matter of fact he has been a bitter disappointment. . . ."

The president could not understand that Wendell might allow the same freedom of operation to industrial combination that he allowed to labor organization. Nor could he appreciate that there might be a difference between Wendell, the judge, and Wendell, the private citizen.

"Roosevelt looked on my dissent to the *National Securities Case* as a political departure," Wendell told Pollock many years later. Of T.R. himself, he added: "He was very likeable, a big figure, a rather ordinary intellect, with extraordinary gifts, a shrewd and I think pretty unscrupulous politican. He played all his cards—if not more. *R.i.p.*"

Although Wendell always kept his distance from partisan matters, he nevertheless felt sufficient identification with his party in 1924 to express satisfaction over Coolidge's victory. It meant that Wendell did not have to worry about the propriety of resigning in order to give the naming of his successor to a Republican president.

Wendell had rejected any opportunity to run for office when such a possibility was advanced by Senator Lodge. Even with this possibility excluded, he confined his public activities to the job in hand and avoided the sort of executive branch intervention which Louis D. Brandeis and Felix Frankfurter later engaged in, the consultation with the executive provided by William Howard Taft, or the manoevering for personal advancement practiced by William O. Douglas. Thus, while he was not a closet Republican, he was never an active participant in political functioning. As with other human pursuits, he was content to view the struggle from afar.

NOTES ON POLITICS

[1]Charles Sumner (1811–1874), antislavery leader, U.S. Senator from Massachusetts (1851–74), one of the founders of the Republican Party. Caned on the floor of the Senate by Rep. Preston Brooks, of South Carolina, a Southern sympathizer.

[2]John A. Garraty (1920–   ), distinguished student of American history, editor: *Dictionary of American Biography*, professor of History at Columbia University.

3 John A. Garraty. "Holmes' Appointment to the United States Supreme Court," *New England Quarterly* XXII:3 (Sept. 1949):85–97.

4 George Frisbie Hoar (1826–1904), U.S. Senator from Massachusetts (1877–1904), son of Rep. Samuel Hoar and father of Rep. Rockwood Hoar. Presided over the Republican National Convention of 1880. Member of potent Massachusetts political family.

5 James Gillespie Blaine (1830–1893), prominent Republican politician, known as the "Plumed Knight," speaker of the House of Representatives (1869–1875), U.S. Senator from Maine, secretary of state under President Garfield. Nominated for president in 1884, but defeated by Grover Cleveland due to "Rum, Romanism and Rebellion" speech by Blaine supporter Rev. Samuel D. Burchard just before the election.

Apologia Pro Vita Sua

Anthony Powell, the British novelist,[1] has observed that each of us creates his own "personal myth" in life, and Wendell was no exception to this rule. He viewed himself as the lonely adventurer climbing to the summit of the highest intellectual peaks where the atmosphere of thought was rarefied and competitors few. As he shrank from broad and vague generalizations in the law, he also did so in formulating his view of the cosmos, as he liked to call it. He termed his prejudices and predilections his "can't helps" and refused to make them universal postulates.

His code was an unusual mixture of skepticism and romanticism. As one who did not *know* the answers, he was an agnostic in the basic sense of the word. His attitude was a Missourian "show me" to those who asserted the validity of a philosophy. He viewed the breaking of the images of the old gods with calm detachment. He distrusted enthusiasts and advocates of causes. While this aloofness governed his approach to questions of broad scope, his view of certain specific phenomena, such as war and legal scholarship, was colored by an almost passionate romanticism.

Wendell was the product of his times. He came to maturity when laissez-faire capitalism was putting into practice on a massive scale the theories preached by Adam Smith. In addition, discoveries in all branches of science were challenging the traditional view of the universe and its development. Charles Darwin published his earthshaking book in 1859 and its full title, *On the Origin of Species by Means of Natural Selection, or the Preservation of Favoured Races in the Struggle for Life,* provided Wendell with language which he often used, while its content colored his speculations about human behavior as well as economic and philosophic development. To the Darwinian influence was added the powerful sway of Thomas Hobbes with his materialism and fascination with power. With the explosion of science and its startling explanation of natural phenomena

131

on the one hand and the simplistic response of the traditional religionists on the other, Wendell found no appeal in organized religion and based his own conclusions about the universe and man's place in the cosmos upon demonstrable fact. Although he was christened and buried through ceremonies in Unitarian churches—and he and Fanny were married in an Episcopal church by a minister of that faith—he never took part in the observances of even this minimally rigid sect.

Wendell's view of life as an arena of contending forces where the stronger prevailed was certainly strengthened by his three years' experience with the brutality of infantry combat in the Civil War whose Union deaths doubled such American losses in World War I, Korea, and Vietnam combined. His self-reliant individualism was permanently solidified in his first battle when he consciously refused to seek traditional solace in the Divinity even though he was badly wounded and thought that he might die. His expression of his rationale, written shortly after his injury, established a position that varied little over the succeeding years.

> Of course when I thought I was dying the reflection that the majority vote of the civilized world declared that with my opinions I was *en route* for Hell came up with painful distinctness— Perhaps the first impulse was tremulous—but then I said—by Jove, I die like a soldier anyhow—I was shot in the breast doing my duty up to the hub—afraid? No, I am proud—then I thought I couldn't be guilty of a deathbed recantation—father and I had talked of that and were agreed that it generally meant nothing but a cowardly giving way to fear—Besides, thought I, can I recant if I want to, has the approach of death changed my beliefs much? & to this I answered—No—Then came in my Philosophy—I am to take a leap in the dark—but now as ever I believe that whatever shall happen is best—for it is in accordance with a general law—and *good & universal* (or *general law*) are synonymous terms in the universe. . . .[2]

Thus, the strength of his convictions was tested in the most challenging way when he was twenty and proved impregnable. The formulation which he adopted, with some variety of expression, remained unchanged through his life.

While dismissing adherence to organized religion for himself, his view of the phenomenon varied in expression, as with all of us, with the identity of the person with whom he was discussing it. With a secretary who was a Catholic, he could sympathize with the civilizing role of the Catholic church and its leadership, on occasion, in encouraging adjustment to changing social conditions, while criticizing its bald manipulation of political power. With another secretary who was not religious, he could praise the beauty in nature and art developed and protected by the church, but attack the inflexibility of its dogma. With Harold Laski, who was anti-Catholic, and expecting anonymity, he could write with savagery of a Catholic book for children "published in this century that talked about Hell," and lament that the "poor little devils" should "hear a puke in an apron trying to scare them stiff with a picture of the Hell they are likely to be sent to. . . ." With Laski, he could also say, ". . . I don't believe in the infinite importance of man—I see no reason to believe that a shudder could go through the sky if the whole ant heap were kerosened. . . ." At the same time, he could say to his friend Canon Sheehan, that "man may have cosmic destinies beyond his ken" and could win from the canon the accolade that Holmes's thinking on the place of the intellect in arriving at truth paralleled that of the dogmatic teaching of the Roman Church. He even went so far as to contribute to the upkeep of the Catholic church in Beverly Farms—for the benefit of the servants in his household. In the final analysis, however, he was irreligious and made rather a pose of it. "I have the same respect for religion," he said, "that I have for the Roman Law or anything else that has historical significance."

He concluded by disclaiming omniscience, concluding that he was "in the belly of the cosmos and not the cosmos in him." Frequently expressed in similarly amusing language, his judgment was "not proven" as to a rational universe and his mechanistic cosmos lacked the consoling presence of a guiding Deity. Drawing on his battle experience he expressed his view of man's situation:

> I think the proper attitude is that we know nothing of cosmic values and bow our heads—seeing reason enough for doing all we can and not demanding the plan of campaign of the General—or even asking whether there is any general or any plan.

It's enough for me that this universe can produce intelligence, ideals, etc.—*et superest ager.*

Above all, to act. In many ways this summed up his philosophy. One should, he said, use one's powers to the utmost. Life was action.

There was no cheer or illusion in his view of the universe. He did make a sort of concession, describing Fabré's "most charming picture of maggots preparing their way for a destiny they did not understand." "If maggots," he added, "why not man?" Canon Sheehan was quick to ask him what were "the ends outside ourselves" which he had spoken of in a speech, but Wendell never answered this question for the canon, or, one suspects, for himself.

His personal experience and his mechanistic view of the universe led him to emphasize and even overemphasize the importance of force in his exegesis of law and order. "I believe that force is the *ultima ratio*," he said in *The Common Law*[3] and, elsewhere, "a right is only the hypostasis of a prophecy— the imagination of a substance supporting the fact that the public force will be brought to bear upon those who do things said to contravene it." "Truth," he said, "was the majority vote of that nation that could lick all others."[4]

Wendell loved to create a pungent phrase and his epigrams were formed to attract attention. It pleased him to shock the bourgeoisie or, as he said, to "make the monkeys howl." With the expression of his views in such form, it is not surprising that they should have aroused passionate and even violent opposition. Among these adversaries, as we have seen, were natural law devotees and formal religionists who accepted revelation, personal Divinity, and the nobility of mankind. They particularly deprecated Wendell's allocation of importance to force in the basis of law and his equating man in the universal scale of significance with a grain of sand or a baboon. His opponents argued that his philosophy would open the way to *Blut und Eisen* standards. These opponents included Henry R. Luce[5] in "Holmes Was Wrong" in *Fortune Magazine* and Harold R. McKinnon[6] in the *American Bar Association Journal.* The attacks were countered by defenders who included Professor Fred Rodell[7] of the Yale Law School, former Attorney General Francis Biddle and Professor Mark DeWolfe Howe.

While Wendell's view of cosmic reality was stark and dour, his conception of the roles of the soldier and the scholar was surprisingly romantic.

"Through our great good fortune, in our youth," Wendell said in one famous speech on Memorial Day in Keene, New Hampshire, in 1884, "our hearts were touched with fire." And the words of the modifying phrase were used with full knowledge of their significance. In spite of his own wounds and physical privations, the incredible carnage of mass battles, the loss of friends and the debasement of the idealism with which he began the war, he considered his role as a soldier to have been a high and admirable one and this opinion remained firm and unchanged to the end of his days. When he completed the three years of enlisted service, his battle-induced physical and nervous condition forced him to decide that he could not resume his military ordeal. After an emotional explanation to his parents, he returned to Boston and civilian life, but the memory of his own experiences and the sufferings and deaths of his companions never prevented him from viewing the soldier's role through a romantic lens.

As Barton Leach put it:

His attitude toward the War was Arthurian. He thought of it as a gallant, heroic, purifying quest.[8] The fact that it maimed young bodies and destroyed young lives was the price to be paid, and it was worth the price. In one of his speeches he said, "I think we all feel that to us at least the War would seem less beautiful and inspiring if those few gentlemen had not died as they did." He always thought of himself as a soldier and of life in terms of battle. I remember him saying, "I always thought that when I reached the age of eighty I could wrap my life up in a scroll, tie a pink ribbon around it, put it away in a drawer and go about doing the things I've always wanted to do. But I learned early in life that when you have taken one trench there is always a new firing line."

He was willing to give public testimony to his noble view of war as he did in his Keene speech where he spoke of those who had "seen with our own eyes, beyond and above the gold fields, the snowy heights of honor." He even marched with other aging veterans in a parade before President Taft at Beverly Farms in 1909 when Wendell was sixty-eight. To Canon

Sheehan he described the marchers as "old fellows with faces twisted by age and work, but alive with the romance of their memories." Certainly these were spiritualized expressions from one who could describe man as a "cosmic ganglion" and to whom "The formula of life to the great masses would be Feed F-*outre* and Finish . . ."

While he was placed upon a pedestal by many liberals in the twenties and thirties, he always made clear that he did not share their antiwar sentiments. One secretary described his attitude: "When young people used to call on him, particularly when Frankfurter was younger and would bring along some bright young things who were in favor of disarmament, and there'd be a group of them in the downstairs living room, Holmes would sometimes say, 'Now I hope you proper geese have left your *proper-ganda* behind.'

"There never was a major anniversary of the war," the secretary continued, "that was not on his mind." This was especially true of the dates of battles where he was wounded. He would head a letter to Pollock with the notation that the date was the anniversary of Ball's Bluff or write to Canon Sheehan that on September seventeenth, he had drunk a glass of wine "to the living and the dead, it being the anniversary of Antietam, where, in 1862–1908—46 years ago (!) I was shot through the neck." In the last years of his life, as we have noted, he regularly visited war-related sites with his secretaries or the ladies who were invited to share his company.

Some of Wendell's memories of the war were grim indeed. "When he mentioned the Seven Days battles," Mark Howe noted in his diary,

> and I asked him whether he had really fought for seven days—he said that he thought they did and that anyway he remembers looking at the sun and saying "God why can't it go down so that we can rest." To show how much he hated war, he described the surgeon of his regiment after he (OWH) was wounded in the heel saying to someone else that Holmes really wanted to lose his foot. And Holmes said to me that he was praying that his foot might be cut off so that he wouldn't have to go back.[9]

Howe summarized Wendell's sentiments about combat: "His feeling about the war was, apparently, while it was going on, one of great horror. He feels that you simply do it because you have to." This characterization was in contrast to that with which he favored the shocked young lady visitors during his convalescence in Boston when he described it as an "organized bore." Probably, both were true.

NOTES ON APOLOGIA PRO VITA SUA

[1] Anthony Powell (1905–   ), distinguished British novelist, author of the twelve volume *roman fleuve, A Dance to the Music of Time,* critic and playwright.

[2] Mark DeWolfe Howe ed.: *Touched With Fire* (Cambridge: Harvard University Press. 1946), pp. 27–28.

[3] Holmes, *The Common Law,* p. 44.

[4] Oliver Wendell Holmes, Jr., "Natural Law," *Harvard Law Review* 32: 40,42 (1918); Oliver Wendell Holmes, Jr., *Collected Legal Papers* (New York: Harcourt, Brace and Company, 1920), pp. 310, 313.

[5] Henry R. Luce (1898–1967), Chinese-born son of American missionaries, Yaleman, founder of *Time,* the weekly newsmagazine, and *Fortune.*

[6] Harold R. McKinnon, "The Secret of Mr. Justice Holmes: An Analysis," 36 *American Bar Association Journal* (April 1950), pp. 261–4; 342–6.

[7] Fred Rodell (1907–1980), longtime professor of law at Yale Law School, humorist, iconoclast and baseball expert. He wrote "Holmes and His Hecklers," *Progressive* 15:4 (April 1951), pp. 9–11.

[8] Perhaps he had something of the feeling of Edwin Arlington Robinson's Miniver Cheevy:

> Miniver loved the days of old
> When swords were bright and steeds were prancing;
> The vision of a warrior bold
> Would set him dancing.

Edwin Arlington Robinson, *Collected Poems* (The Macmillan Company 1922.), p. 347.

[9] Mark De Wolfe Howe, unpublished diary in possession of Harvard Law School Library, p. 23.

The Resignation

Wendell's ninetieth birthday brought recognition on an international scale. The Lord Chancellor and the attorney general of Great Britain had written about it. Judge Cardozo, Walter Lippmann, John Dewey, and Felix Frankfurter had noticed it. The peak of the observance was a national broadcast arranged for that Sunday evening. Dean Charles E. Clark, of the Yale Law School and the president of the American Bar Association spoke from New York and Chief Justice Charles E. Hughes spoke from Washington. In Cambridge, five hundred people gathered in the court room of Langdell Hall at the Harvard Law School to hear the broadcast. Wendell spoke into a microphone set on his desk at his home on I (Eye) Street. His voice was low, but clear and resonant:

> In this symposium my part is only to sit in silence. To express my feelings as the end draws near is too intimate a task.
>
> But I may mention one thought that comes to me as a listener-in. The riders in a race do not stop short when they reach the goal. There is a little finishing canter before coming to a standstill. There is time to hear the kind voices of friends and to say to one's self: "The work is done." But just as one says that, the answer comes: "The race is over, but the work never is done while the power to work remains." The canter that brings you to a standstill need not be only coming to rest. It cannot be while you still live. For to live is to function. That is all there is in living.
>
> And so I end with a line from a Latin poet who uttered the message more than fifteen hundred years ago:—
>
> "Death plucks my ear and says, Live—I am coming."

Wendell's use of the quotation evoked a pedantic response from his great correspondent Sir Frederick Pollock as to its attribution[1] which Wendell airily dismissed by a return letter of May 15, 1931. Pollock thought that Wendell had inappropriately used a "pseudo-Virgilian *Copa*" or wine toast.

Alger Hiss, Wendell's secretary in 1929–1930, remembers

the judge asking him to let him know if the younger man ever saw any "signs of slippage." The secretary said he never saw any symptoms that warranted notification. Although Wendell always told a new secretarial appointee that he reserved the right to die or retire during the term of the secretary's employment, up to this time there had never been any indication that either option would be exercised. In 1930 and 1931, however, a gradual deterioration became apparent; by the time H. Chapman Rose became the secretary in 1932, the situation had reached a disturbing level. Wendell was still on the Court and, even though the other justices compensated for this debility, there remained an inescapable minimum of personal obligations. Rose worked fifteen-hour days simply because someone had to be on hand to minister to Wendell's needs. Rose became increasingly worried as Wendell's native will to work struggled against his growing fatigue, resulting in nervous exhaustion. Unknown to either, the Supreme Court justices, concerned about Wendell's condition, had discussed what could be done about the situation.

Rose became aware of these conversations when Chief Justice Hughes telephoned to make an appointment to see Wendell at home on Sunday morning, January 10, 1932. Hughes arrived at 10:30 or 11:00, and Rose continues the story:

> The chief justice went up to Justice Holmes's study on the second floor and they conversed there for a time—I should think about a half hour and then sent for me. My assignment was to pull out from the shelves of the library the volume of the statutes that had to do with tenure and retirement and find the place which dealt with the subject—which I did and gave it to them. Then, I left and waited downstairs as I had been before. Then, after another interval—and I'll never forget the sight—the chief justice walked down the stairs with tears just streaming down his face—a remarkable sight on that impressive face with its white mustache and beard.
>
> He left and I went upstairs to see the justice. I found Mary Donnellan kneeling at his feet in tears. He was then and thereafter totally stoic about it. There was no expression of emotion one way or the other. Then, within fifteen minutes, Justice Brandeis arrived and spent perhaps an hour with him, obviously by arrangement.

SUR LE RETOUR. Wendell's last portrait taken by Clara E. Sipprell in December 1934.

Mary Donnellan, who received the news so emotionally, supports the picture of Wendell's stoicism, but has a further analysis of his feelings: "Even though his heart was breaking, he wouldn't let anyone know. He was that kind. He didn't want to resign. He tried to hold on, but I guess he was a little more feeble. He wasn't sad and he wasn't glad. He was lonesome and he thought that was the end." Mary's loyalty prevented her hot resentment from cooling entirely even after the passage of fifty years until she was interviewed. She did not feel sympathy for Hughes in the difficult ministerial act which he was called upon to perform. "Chief Justice Hughes was very cold," she said, reprovingly.

On January eleventh, Wendell delivered his last opinion in the Court—his voice so faint that it could scarcely be heard beyond the first row of seats. When Court adjourned on that day, he walked over to the clerk's desk and said, "I won't be down tomorrow." That same day, he wrote and sent his resignation to the president to take effect on the next day. On that next day, the remaining justices wrote to Wendell and sent their note around by messenger, a valedictory composition such as he had performed for the Court upon Taft's resignation. He replied:

> My Dear Brethren:
> You must let me call you so once more. Your more than kind, your generous letter, touches me to the bottom of my heart. The long and intimate association with men who so command my respect and admiration could not but fix my affection as well. For such little time as may be left for me I shall treasure it as adding gold to the sunset.
>
> > Affectionately yours,
> > Oliver Wendell Holmes

On Tuesday, January 12, 1932 for the first time in forty-nine years, Wendell was not an active member of a court of law.

NOTE ON THE RESIGNATION

[1] Howe, *Holmes-Pollock Letters*, vol. 2, p. 285.

Sur Le Retour

Wendell was eighty-eight when Fanny died and in his remaining six years of life, there was an expected and gradual diminution of his powers. This weakening became especially apparent after his resignation from the Court in 1932. His mind remained clear. He retained his appetite for food, but his step became insecure and his voice lost its deep, musical resonance. With Mary policing, he limited his cigars to two a day, except for an occasional "toot." His body lost its military erectness and he developed a marked stoop. He found it difficult to straighten up when he rose from his chair and he required the services of Mary and a secretary to raise him into position. "It gets harder to open up the jack-knife," he said.

He continued his reading sessions, sometimes with relays of lectors, finding solace in the rolling sound of the words. He followed the texts carefully, however, and commented or asked questions about matters that seized his interest. Nevertheless, there were times when he would fall into a reverie or drop into a brief doze.

Still, he had his visitors, mostly female and in the upper age brackets, with a few younger women to keep him up on gossip and current topics. Mary, the secretary, Charlie Buckley, and the rest of the staff kept an eye on him and supplied his wants. Nearly every day he would have his secretary call one of his young lady friends, or he would invite the secretary himself, and Charlie would be summoned to bring around the car. They would then go off for a ride into the Virginia countryside or into the "free state" of Maryland.

Although Wendell no longer had formal duties, he continued to employ a "secretary," still selected by Felix Frankfurter from the cream of the top class at the Harvard Law School. After his resignation, his aides were: Chappie Rose, Donnie Hiss, Mark Howe, and Jim Rowe. Rowe came on board in the fall of 1934. He enjoyed his association with Wendell—even though he received more information about the Civil War than he cared to

143

absorb at that time. Still, he found it "fun" to be with the old man, except when they embarked on some dull reading which could not be laid aside. He enjoyed the automobile rides, too, with the accompanying commentary from Wendell.

On a bitterly cold day—February 23, 1935—they went out for what would be their last drive. The next morning, Wendell had a cold which turned into pneumonia, then called "the old man's friend." In those days, as Rowe said, if you were old and got pneumonia, "you just slipped off into a coma and died." The miraculous sulfa drugs were not yet in common use. Every day, Wendell declined a bit more. As the end grew near, Mary, in concern for the soul of her beloved employer and friend, sprinkled a few drops of water over his head in baptism— although the effect may have been problematical since he had already been baptized as an infant.

Finally, a huge oxygen tank was brought into the bedroom and a tent was lifted over his face. Although Wendell dozed fitfully, there were still moments when the storied humor was apparent. Shortly before Wendell died, Frankfurter, one of the last to see him alive, bent over the bed. Wendell opened his eyes and, even though he could not speak, brought his hand as close as he could to his face and thumbed his nose at Frankfurter. Thus he met death with unconcern. Death came at two in the morning of March sixth, two days before his ninety-fourth birthday.

Taps for the Captain

Wendell's funeral would have pleased him and made him proud. It was a ceremonial affair with full military honors befitting one with his distinguished combat record. He was buried on what would have been his ninety-fourth birthday, March 8, 1935, a day of excruciatingly bad weather.

The funeral ceremony took place at All Souls Unitarian Church at the top of Sixteenth Street in Washington. A corps of Wendell's secretaries acted as ushers and as pallbearers, carrying the flag-draped casket into the church. The pulpit was banked with flowers which included a large wreath of roses from the White House and a huge spray of roses and lilies of the valley from the justices of the Supreme Court. Many dignitaries attended to pay their respects. Among those present were Vice-President Garner, members of the Cabinet, Mrs. Franklin D. Roosevelt, Mrs. Woodrow Wilson, Mrs. Charles Evans Hughes, officials of the executive and legislative branches of the government, delegations of the Congress, the diplomatic corps and the American Bar Association, and seven of the nine members of the Supreme Court. Absent were Justices Brandeis and Van Devanter whose age forbade them to test the inclement weather. Several hundred members of the public "braved the chill wind and blowing flurries of snow to stand outside the church," the *Boston Evening Transcript* reported. For some reason, seats for the public were limited and they were not admitted to the church even though, according to John Knox, the Illinois Holmes scholar, there was a "waste of space which I regretted."

The musical program, selected by Tommy Corcoran, included the largos from Handel's *Xerxes* and from Dvorak's *New World Symphony,* as well as music of Bach, Chopin, and Franck.

The Reverend Ulysses G. B. Pierce, D.D., conducted the service. He read a brief excerpt from Scripture and two other selections. The first was an excerpt from an address Wendell had delivered on the death of Chief Justice Walbridge A. Field of Massachusetts in 1899: "We accept our destiny to work, to fight, to die for ideal aims. At the grave of a hero who has done these things, we end, not with sorrow at the inevitable loss, but with the contagion of his courage, and with a kind of desperate joy, we go back to the fight."

He could have found no more appropriate words for himself.

The other reading was a poem which must have been a favorite of Wendell and Fanny since he had read it at Fanny's funeral service. It was called "To Night" or "Night and Death" and was written by a fabulous character called Jose Maria Blanco y Crespa. He was born in Spain, became a Roman Catholic priest, left the church, spurned Christianity, went to England, became an Anglican, changed his name to Joseph Blanco White, played the violin with John Henry Newman, left the Anglican fold, became a Unitarian and wrote pamphlets such as *The Poor Man's Preservative Against Popery*. His literary fame was said to have been based upon one sonnet. At one time, the poem read at the service was included in *the Oxford Book of English Verse:*

> Mysterious Night! When our first parent knew
> Thee from report divine, and heard thy name,
> Did he not tremble for this lovely frame,
> This glorious canopy of light and blue?
> Yet 'neath a curtain of translucent dew,
> Bathed in the rays of the great setting flame,
> Hesperus with the host of heaven came,
> And lo! Creation widened in man's view.
> Who could have thought such darkness lay concealed
> Within thy beams, O Sun! or who could find,
> Whilst fly and leaf and insect stood revealed,
> That to such countless orbs thou mad'st us blind!
>   Why do we then shun death with anxious strife?
>   If Light can thus deceive, wherefore not Life?

At Arlington National Cemetery, the coffin was placed upon a caisson, drawn by artillery horses, and accompanied by a guard of honor. The Army Band played "The Battle Hymn of the Republic," and the riderless horse with boots reversed in the stirrups walked in the procession. At the grave, activity was suspended while President Roosevelt, with Mrs. Roosevelt at his side, slowly made his way from his car in the cold and sleet to stand bare-headed in tribute. Dr. Pierce spoke the words of the Twenty-third Psalm, and a triple volley was fired by the honor guard. The bugler sounded "Taps," and then the casket was lowered into the ground. At this point, a low-flying plane thundered overhead as it rose from the nearby airport, symbolizing for Knox "the spirit of Holmes taking leave into the unknown."

Jim Rowe, the last secretary, and Mary Donnellan, the housekeeper, had shared a car and stood together at the grave. Writing to Felix Frankfurter two weeks after the funeral, Rowe summed it all up with grace and sensitivity. Saying that all who had written about Wendell had "quoted Mr. Justice Holmes about himself," he added: "To be a bit different, I shall quote our friend Mary who loved him so devotedly, because I think she came as close to saying what I feel sure he would have felt about it all as anyone I know. I think he would have smiled with pleasure at not the least apt of his students when she stood in the rain as the soldiers took him off the caisson. As she watched him being carried past her she merely said: 'Soldiers don't mind the rain.'"

A fitting epitaph.

CURRICULUM VITAE

A native of Waterbury, Connecticut, John S. Monagan was educated at Dartmouth College and Harvard Law School. He practiced law in Waterbury and Washington for twenty-seven years and served five years as mayor of Waterbury and seven terms as a member of Congress from Connecticut's Fifth District.

Monagan's book reviews and writings on historical and political subjects have appeared in a variety of publications. He is the author of *Horace: Priest of the Poor,* a biography of a Washington inner-city priest.

He is a devotee of good music, plays the piano and has been a member of many choral groups. He and his wife, Rosemary, a musician and archaeologist, live in Georgetown, D.C. They have five children and four grandsons.

Index